Here Come
The Gypsies

Here Come The Gypsies

The Tales Of A Wandering Educator

Harvey P. Getz

PARTRIDGE

To order additional copies of this book, contact
Toll Free 800 101 2657 (Singapore)
Toll Free 1 800 81 7340 (Malaysia)
orders.singapore@partridgepublishing.com

www.partridgepublishing.com/singapore

"Memoirs means when you put down the good things you ought to have done and leave out the bad you did do."

~Will Rogers

My wife and I were walking around Florence taking pictures of the Piazza della Republica, Michelangelo's David, the Duomo, and the Ponte Vecchio, an ancient bridge that provided a perfect way to cross over the River Arno. The danger alert sounded when I noticed that heading in our direction was a band of gypsies. I immediately noted that one of the girls had a newspaper in her hand, and it wasn't because she was interested in finding out what was going on in the world. Instead, it was the shield that hid the heist before they handed the loot off to some unknown person or persons. The thought of losing my wallet, video camera, and anything else the thieving girls could get their hands on was a disaster in the making. *How is it that I have so much stuff? I remember when there was a time when I had nothing worth stealing. Now, I am worried that a bunch of gypsy girls are going to rob me.* I knew that I had to do something quick, not only for myself, but also for my wife who was walking next to me. She was anticipating the attack by wrapping her leather purse tightly around her slender arm. But as I quickly put together my plan for defending what was rightfully ours, I thought back to those simpler times when I really didn't have anything to steal. My childhood experiences, my friends, my wife, and my world travels led me down the path to a comfortable middle class life. I suppose the best place to start is at the beginning of my story, then follow the antiquated path through my childhood, and continue on the trail of life until I reach the present time.

Altoona, Pennsylvania

The morning sun danced between the clouds causing the elongated shadows of Mother and me to play hide and seek on the cracked and uneven sidewalk. In spite of the war, the two of us temporarily set aside all the cares in the world as we made our way to downtown Altoona. Considering the condition the world was in at that time, things didn't seem to be all that bad, especially since my dad, and some of my uncles and cousins were in the service helping to win the war against the Germans and Japanese. My two brothers were home with Aunt Ann, and because I liked having mother to myself once in a while, I grabbed her hand and gave it a little squeeze.

I was only a little kid, but I was old enough to recognize that Mother was a pretty lady. The soldiers and sailors' frequent glances were a sign that she was a peach of a woman. During our walks down Eighteen Street, whenever a serviceman walked up the street and snuck a peep at mother, I would make a tiny fist, not where anyone could see it, but because I was too small and skinny to get into fight, especially with a soldier, but I did it just in case he tried something.

Looking up at her pretty face, I asked, "Mom, can we go to Walgreen's for a piece of pie after we're finished?"

Shifting her purse from her arm to her hand, she replied, "If you are good boy, I'll think about it."

Finally reaching the center of the city, after walking past the Bell Telephone office, Dr. "Painless" Krishner's dental office, Traub's toy store, and a half dozen other shops, we reached our destination. It was the block-long and block-wide Gables Department Store. It was so big, that it even had its own radio station, WFBG. Not only was it the largest commercial building in Altoona, it was the biggest department store this side of Pittsburgh. We walked a block down the hill to the main entrance, and that is when we saw the long line of waiting women.

"Well, Harvey, it looks like I'm going to be here for a while. But I'm telling you, I'm really tired of having Aunt Ann paint lines down the back of my legs, so let's hope for the best."

The "best" was getting two pairs of nylon stockings before Gable's depleted their supply of the precious items. They were a rationed item making it difficult, if not impossible, to obtain unless the store had gotten the stockings to distribute to the patient women. People had victory gardens to grow supplies of vegetables, and collected old pots and pans to melt down for bullets, but things like gasoline, meat, and nylon stockings, were almost impossible to get anywhere.

While shifting her purse to her left arm, Mother seemed lost in her thoughts about the nylons, but I asked her anyway. "Hey Mother, would it be okay if I go inside Gables and look around for a little while?"

Staring at the long line ahead of her, she nodded her head and replied, "All right, but don't get lost, and don' t touch anything. And be back here in a half an hour," she warned.

Thinking about the possibility of cherry pie when we were finished shopping, I replied, "OK, Mother, I promise I won't be late."

Roaming through the gigantic store, I saw many amazing things that were a treat to my eyes. On the ground floor, there were shirts, ties, shoes, pants, suits, hats, and stuff that any man would be proud to wear. The second floor displayed dresses and ladies wear that would delight any woman rich enough to afford them. Walking up to the third level, I saw toys that delighted me, and a couple of record booths where people listened to Dinah Shore, Frank Sinatra, Duke Ellington, Glenn Miller, or whoever they fancied.

The thirty minutes flew by faster than a P-51, so I ran back to mother, who was still waiting in the long line of hopeful women. "It looks like it's going to take longer than I thought," she lamented.

Mother was a bit frustrated, but remained as determined as the early bird is to a worm. "I'm gonna' stay here for as long as it takes. She added with some regret, "even if I have to wait here all day."

I looked at the line ahead of us, "Yep. The line is still pretty long all right."

"It sure is," Mother replied.

Then I asked, "Mom is it OK if I wandered around town a bit? I promise to be back in a half an hour."

"Well, all right," she answered, "but don't be late."

As fast as my little legs could carry me, I ran past men with dirty faces wearing bibbed overalls and stripped railroad caps that looked like the ones the marines wore. Altoona, at the time, was home to the world's largest railroad yards where thousands of skilled employees worked. Among them were master mechanics who built and repaired trains and railroad cars for the Pennsylvania Railroad. So important were the shops, that three Nazi spies were captured just before they blew up a section of the nearby Horseshoe Curve. Besides the people wearing suits or dresses, I also saw miners with carbide lamps attached to their hard hats, and most of them wore clothes badly in need of a good washing.

Finally, I was at McCroys where I spent fifteen minutes wandering around the store before going next door to Kresses. The counters in both the places looked like they had been waiting for me to explore the mysteries that delighted this seven-year old kid. Watches, jewelry, school, and office supplies were on the first floor. In the basement were such things as kaleidoscopes, yo-yos, games, and all kinds of toys, including bicycles. But best of all, there were toy cowboy pistols and rifles. I picked up and held the guns regardless of what my mother had warned me not to do. Besides, the women working behind the counter didn't seem to mind at all.

Because time was running short, I decided to skip Woolworth's. Like the scores of other death- defying jaywalkers, I darted across busy Eleven Avenue, where cars zipped by honking their horns, streetcars sparked electricity from the overhanging wires, and buses spewed plumes of exhaust from their tail pipes, to see what was playing at the Capital Theatre. The featured presentation for the week was *Meet Me In St. Louis*, starring Judy Garland. Altoona's downtown had six movie theaters, not including the one out in Mansion Park, but this was the closest one to Gables Department Store. There were a few other big stores in town like Kaufman's and the Bon Ton, but I didn't have time to go to those places. Instead, I crossed the street to Gables just in time to meet mother as she was coming out of the store with a couple of pairs of nylons.

"Well, I got them!" She had a wonderful smile on her handsome face. Then she teased, "Now let me see, where should we go now?"

"Can we go to Walgreens for a piece of pie?" I pleaded.

She smiled, "OK. And we'll even get some ice cream on it!" She declared.

We sat at the counter in Walgreens and enjoyed our cherry pie with vanilla ice cream on top. Before leaving the drug store, I walked to the back of the shop to admire what they had in stock. There were toys, flashlights, camping gear, household items, candy, and a collection of other items. The stores were like museums to me. You looked at the toys and other things, but owning them was out of the question.

On our way home, a soldier marched past us looking as if he was going off to war. His eyes were focused on what was ahead of him, and his shoulders were straight as a rod.

I didn't make a fist this time.

Garfield Elementary School

Walking to school five days a week wasn't without risk for a Jewish kid living in Altoona's Fifth Ward. Two blocks down from my house, just past my favorite chestnut tree where I collected dozens of beautiful chestnuts in the fall, was a Gulf gas station. As I walked by, a couple of wise guys who worked there made their usual unsolicited remarks about Jews. But I let it go because they were pretty big fellows, and there was nothing a little kid could do about it anyway. Just as I was recovering from their bonehead comments on Judaism, I turned the corner and headed into that god-forsaken place called, "Polish Alley."

Confined to this very narrow street were small concrete houses mortared together so there wasn't an inch of space between them. The row of drab single-story tiny dwellings continued in the same monotonous manner for nearly a city block. Staring at me with accusing eyes from across the alleyway was the Polish school and Catholic Church. After all, I had killed their savior and the Poles weren't going to let me forget it. Because I was the only Jew stupid enough to enter their territory, like clockwork, they waited every morning to bombard me with jeers and derisive comments in the Polish language. They must have shouted out some very funny things because they certainly got big laughs out of them. After running the gauntlet of Poles, and thankfully the only word I understood was, Zyd, which means "Jew" in English, and enduring the wise cracks from the Laurel and Hardy demagogues, I ran through a vacant lot and onto Sixteen Street before heading up a hill that was next to the Polish National Alliance, a beer drinking club. Finally, making a left turn just a few yards passed the PNA, I started my climb up the eroded escarpment that ended just one block from my school.

Without feelings or a heart, staring back at me like a colossal beast was Garfield Elementary School. The two story, red brick structure reached up into the sky to destroy whatever creativity it could find in the heavens. The dreaded concrete bathroom in the basement of the school was like a large dungeon where a whole class of boys lined up to piss at one time. Mr. Breckenridge, who had been a janitor at the school forever, sped things up by swiping the kids on their little butts with a big stick. Knowing what was about to happen, I always managed to get in the far end of the line of peeing boys to avoid the smacks. The interior of the school was in pretty bad shape. We couldn't use the back steps that led up to the second floor because they might collapse if a whole class walked on them. As for the classrooms, they had large windows that allowed the promise of eventual freedom to shine on the mostly disinterested students. The boys and girls sat silently at their mounted desks praying that they wouldn't get called on to answer any questions. Because fear was paramount, we wanted to remain as invisible and detached as humanly possible. Just about everything in the room was made of oak, including the doors, the floors, the huge closets where we were confined to when we failed to come up with the correct answers, the teacher's paddle, and the lift-up desks with ink holes drilled into them. There was a clock on the wall with a bell system attached that announced the beginning of school, recess, lunch times, and mercifully, the end of school.

Heaven help the student who was late for school or failed to get back from recess before the bell finished ringing, because if he was tardy, corporal punishment was the price he paid.

Because I seldom paid attention to what the teachers were saying, I remember very little about what was happening in the classroom. To be perfectly honest, I was completely bored out of my cotton-picking mind, and instead of listening to my teachers talk about stuff that really didn't interest me, I was off fighting Indians, or flying P-47's against the Germans and Japanese.

All right boys. Bogies at 11 o'clock. I shouted through my radio as my wingman peeled off to meet the Messerschmitt 109's. Rat! tat! tat! tat! My guns were blazing as I tore into one of the Nazis' planes. Take that you dirty rat! Look out Smitty! There's a 109 coming in on your right. Good one, Smitty. We battled in the air for who knows how long. Anyway, it was long enough to last the whole mathematics lesson before I ordered, *OK, boys. Let's head back home.*

Men, we are going to make a stand right here. Corporal, take the horses behind the rocks and stay with them, I commanded. Here they come sir, shouted the sergeant. Bam! Bam! Bam! Our angry Winchesters barked as we cut down the savages with uncanny accuracy. Bam! Bam! Bam! What few Indians that were still alive retreated back into the hills to lick their wounds. Good job, men. Corporal, get the horses. I climbed back onto my horse, put my rifle back into the saddle holster, then I yelled, All right men, saddle up. By twos, let's head back to the fort. Forward, Ho!

Old Memories

Some memories will never be forgotten. Like my first trip to the dentist with Dr. Krishner, or my very first day of school and when Betty Krider peed a yellow stream down the middle of the mounted desks. Some of those early recollections included listening to the radio, particularly the various shows that dominated the airwaves at the time. The Lone Ranger, Tom Mix, Gene Autry, The Shadow, The Green Hornet, The Lux Mystery Theatre, Captain Winslow, and Sergeant Preston of the Northwest Mounted Police, were among my favorite shows. At night, I would lie in bed and listen to stations as far away as South Carolina to such greats as Dinah Shore, Margaret Whiting, and the Les Brown Band.

The day the Allied Forces landed at Normandy, June 6, 1944, I was at Garfield School when the principal played the radio newscast of the invasion over the public address system. It was a time of mixed emotions and heavy hearts, but I was certain that victory would eventually be ours.

The death of Franklin D. Roosevelt was an event that will remain with me forever. It was a spring day in April when we heard on the radio that our thirty-second president of the United States had died of a stroke. After hearing the sad news, mother sent me out to buy a loaf of Stroehmann's bread at the Polish grocery store. As I walked down Eighteen Street, I noted that the road was as deserted as a western ghost town; most of the people remained inside their homes silently mourning our fallen president. Even our neighbor's dog, a Scottie, who always barked at me when I walked by his house, merely stared out the window without so much as a whimper.

We had dropped two atomic bombs on Japan, and the horrible struggle in the Pacific had finally ended. At last, our boys were coming home. Hundreds of cars drove in circles around Eleven and Twelve Avenues with horns blasting away and everybody hanging out of their car windows shouting and waving in joyous celebration of VJ Day.

The Wooden Paddle

Taking no guff from any kid or parent was our iron-fisted principal, Miss Patrice. When the boys were given a whipping, their parents had better not find out about it. If they did, a second beating was in store for the youngsters. The white-haired teacher was in charge of the school, but without a doubt, Miss Brubaker, my fourth grade teacher, was the meanest instructor at Garfield Elementary School. One day, and there were many others just like it, Tom Shoupe, Richard Kringle, and I came into Miss Brubaker's class a couple of seconds after the recess bell had sounded. She was very angry with the three of us, and that is when she declared that we would be punished that afternoon. Since we had been through it many times before, we knew exactly what that meant. Tom, Richard, and I were going to bend over and touch our toes while Miss Brubaker, with more than just a touch of sadism, would smack us across our butts with a rather large wooden paddle. But that wouldn't happen until sometime in the afternoon. She always arranged the schedule for her beatings after lunch. That way, we had plenty of time to think about it. But it also gave us time to prepare for the whipping.

After running home for a dish of Chef Boyardee spaghetti, I went up to my room and put on another pair of trousers underneath the corduroys that I wore that morning. I followed up the insulation of my butt with yesterday's edition of the Altoona Mirror, our local newspaper, and I ate a raw onion to keep the teacher from getting too close. When I got back to school, I checked with Tom and Richard, and they had done the same thing, including eating onions. My guess was that we were as prepared as possible for the paddling. In the middle of the afternoon, just after the geography class, we were called up in front of the class and told to touch our toes. Miss Brubaker whacked each of us three times, CRACK! CRACK! CRACK! But thanks to the additional padding of the extra pairs of pants and the newspapers, it really didn't hurt. However, we shed a few tears just so she wouldn't find out about our trick.

The Patrol Boy

Ever since I was in the fifth grade, I wanted to be a proud member of the school safety patrol, so I asked Miss Patrice if I could be a patrol boy.

As clear as if were yesterday, she challenged, "When you get A's instead of D's in spelling, I will put you on the safety patrol."

This meant that I had the privilege of standing outside in the rain or snow and safely direct kids across the street proudly wearing my white belt and silver badge. I dreamt about that shiny badge and hoped that someday I'd get to wear it. Two weeks later, I earned an "A" on my spelling test, and true to her word, I was put on the school safety patrol.

When our school safety patrol went to Washington for the Patrol Boy Jamboree, we met our congressman, James Van Zandt, and toured the nation's capital. It was one of the best times of my elementary school days, and one of the things that I remember best about the jamboree was that we ate fried chicken, mashed potatoes, corn, pie, and ice cream at the United States Naval Headquarters.

Never had I eaten so well in my entire life.

The Eighteen Street Gang

Although my school days were a bit foggy, what stands out clearly in my mind was the Eighteen Street gang. My brother Lou (he was "Snooky" in those days) and I hung out with the boys when we weren't in school. Every group had its leader, and ours was Eugene Shumaker. He was one of those guys who did everything well. Eugene made the best rubber gum band guns, could throw anything farther, and hit a ball better than any other guy by a country mile. What's a rubber gum band gun? Well, the main body of the gun was a piece of wood that measured approximately nine inches long by five inches wide. A nail was used as part of the trigger assembly. The part of the contraption that made the thing into a gun was two pieces of cut out rubber strips from an inner tube. The other part of the trigger was one-half of a wooden clothespin. The ammunition was a knotted strip of rubber tubing that was fired from the gun. Eugene's "bullets" really stung when they hit their target, and he never missed. That is the reason why everybody wanted to be on his side when we played war.

We also had a football team, but we didn't have a coach. Oh, Joe's dad, Mr. O'Connor, once bought us sweatshirts with green lettering to let the other teams our know who we were, but he never attempted to coach the Eighteen Street Steamrollers. They didn't have Pop Warner or any organized football leagues at that time, so it was just a bunch of kids getting together to play football games in vacant lots around Altoona. Ronnie Rae, my brother, and I weren't very good, so we always played the line.

According to an old Sicilian proverb, "If you have revenge in mind, dig two graves." Well, I had revenge in mind, but I didn't dig two graves. Instead, I helped dig a snow fort directly across from the entrance to the Polish school. Eugene, Donnie Shumaker, who was Eugene's brother, Joe O'Connor, Snooky, and I, made stacks of snowballs while laying in wait for the Poles to end their school day. Finally, the bell rang and the students began filing out of their school. The first kid didn't get five steps from the door before the barrage began. Eugene hit the guy square in the face, and a couple of seconds later, the second fellow also ended up with a snowball in his kisser. The rest of the screaming Poles retreated back into the safety of their school. Every few minutes a brazen soul would try to make a break for it, but he was plastered with snowballs, and as quick as a flash, he would run back inside their sanctuary. Finally, what seemed like an eternity, but it was only a minute or two after the last Pole had tried to make a break for it, that another misguided soul headed through the door. True to form, eagle-eyed Eugene unloaded with another barrage of snowballs. But this time it wasn't a student, it was a nun. The angry woman didn't retreat like the others, but stood her ground even though she had what was left of a couple of snow balls running down her black habit.

"Holy cow, Eugene, you just hit a nun!" I yelled.

"Sweet sufferin' Jesus. I hit a nun!" The poor woman was still covered in snow as she cursed the miscreant boys who had hit her with a snowball. We heard her unholy curses as we fled for our worthless lives up Sixteen Street.

Our gang was not without its sense of literature. Inane as it might have been, when a guy was feeling low, he was treated to at least one of the following poems. This one was titled, "Worms Are Greasy.

> *Worms are greasy,*
> *Slide down easy,*
> *I'm gonna' go out and eat some worms.*
> *Big, juicy slimy ones,*
> *Intsey, tinsey, tiny, ones.*
> *Worms are greasy,*
> *Slide down easy.*
> *I'm gonna' go out and eat some worms.*

The other one had to do with life and the unfairness that sometimes accompanies it.

> *Life's tough.*
> *What's life?*
> *Life is a magazine.*

How much?
Ten cents.
Only got a nickel.
That's tough.
What's tough?
Life's tough.

Indeed, we instinctively relied on a sense of literacy on those rare occasions, even if they were limited to a couple of homespun poems. On the other hand, we were really a nice bunch of guys who cared about each other, especially when a guy was a little down on himself.

The Home Library

Her name has long been forgotten, but I'll always remember the woman who lived just outside the dark shadows of Garfield Elementary School. It was a pleasant spring day when one of my friends, Joey Hunter, was talking about some woman who lived just a few blocks from the school.

"Hey Joey. What are you guys talking about?" I asked without trying to be too nosy.

"Awe, this lady runs a library from her house," Joey answered as he completed his last loop on his yo-yo.

"Really?" I was amazed that some woman would lend out her books. "I've never heard of such a thing before," I said.

"Yep. She opens her library every Thursday," Joey replied.

"I heard about the place, too," said Meryl Martin.

It was Friday, so I had plenty of time to think about the library. In fact, it was nearly long enough to keep me from daydreaming in class. Nevertheless, I still managed to tune out the teacher by flying over Germany and Japan in my P-51, and fighting bloodthirsty Indians. Finally, it was Thursday, and I was going to the woman's house to see if she really lent out books merely for the asking.

Surrounded by flowers, a manicured lawn, and neatly trimmed hedges, I walked slowly up to the front door of the two-story wooden house. After hesitating for a moment, I knocked on the door and a very pleasant looking middle-aged woman, with dark brown eyes and wearing a blue dress that was tailored to fit her slim body, answered the door.

"May I help you, young man?" Her smile lit up the doorway, and her silver hair glowed as brilliantly as a firefly or one of those small flashlights my brother and I bought at Rushall's drugstore for ten cents.

"Uh," I stammered, "I understand that you have boo...books to loan to anyone who wants to read them." Although it was a cool day, I was sweating up a storm.

"I certainly do. Why don't you come in and I'll take you down to the library," she said.

With a pleasant smile on her oval face, she led me down the steps to her basement. Amazed by what I my eyes revealed was a large collection of books lining the entire four walls of the basement.

"Look around and take your time," she said. "After you've selected your book, I'll check it out for you."

"Thank you, ma'am," I answered. I was beginning to feel a little less nervous about being there.

"Young man. Do you go to Garfield School or to St. Leo's?"

"I go to Garfield," I said.

"That's nice. I hope everything is going well for you."

It wasn't, but I did my best to avoid talking about school. After thumbing my way through several books, I picked out an orange-covered book with the title, "The Mystery of the Clown."

"Yes, that certainly is a wonderful book. I know you're going to enjoy it. Indeed, that is a really an excellent choice," she said. She kindly reminded me not to forget that the book is due back next Thursday.

After thanking her, I ran all the way home so that I could start reading it. The story was more than just good. It was great! I finished the book in just two days and I couldn't wait until next Thursday to get another one. A month later, the woman was allowing me to check out three books a week.

Many moons have come and gone since I first walked into that wonderful woman's home library, but I'll always give a special thanks to the lady who introduced me to the joy of reading.

Irving "Butch" Kaminski

My cousin, Irving "Butch" Kaminski, was also a student at Garfield Elementary School, and on many occasions he found himself in trouble with the Jew-baiters who marched up from St. Leo's School to spread the gospel with at least three pairs of knuckle sandwiches. I had my problems, but I handled them by taunting the gang whenever it was my turn to get hassled. I claimed to have killed Jesus, and I told them that he was turning green in the basement of my house. This was the trigger that set off the gang of crusaders to begin their deadly chase. Easily outrunning them to my greatest ally, the steep and eroded hill, it wasn't long before the angry Catholics were tumbling down the hill after being tripped up by its numerous gullies and holes. By the time I reached the bottom of the hill, the threat to my health was history.

Anyway, back to Butch. It was a bit odd that my cousin would come to me for help every time a few guys threatened to beat him up, but I would walk him down the steep Fourteen Avenue hill to keep the Catholic boys from making mince meat out of my cousin. This was the same guy, however, who picked a fight with me almost everyday after Hebrew School.

Although the sessions seemed to drag on forever, Hebrew School was finally over for the day, and as we walked down Fourteen Avenue to the corner of Eighteen Street, Butch pulled out a piece of the unwrapped kosher salami that was tucked away in his pants pocket.

"Have a piece of salami," he offered.

"No, thanks. I'm gonna' eat supper as soon as I get home," I replied.

Suddenly, as if lightning had struck him, or an electric light had been turned off, he became as hostile as a mountain lion in a sheep pen.

"OK, Harv. Put your dukes up, 'cause I'm gonna' hit you," he said.

"Awe come on, Butch. You know you are going to try and hit me, and I'm not gonna' let you do that."

"Put your dukes up and get ready to fight," he warned.

"Look," I explained, "it always goes the same way. You try to hit me, but I slug you first. Then you run home and tell your mother that I hit you again. After hearing your sad story, your mom calls my mom to complain about me. So why don't we forget about it and stay friends?"

Refusing to listen to reason, Butch telegraphed his punch just before taking a swing at me. But, as usual, I hit him first. It wasn't a hard punch, but it was enough to keep him away from me.

"Hey, you hit me!" He acted like it was unexpected in spite of it being an almost daily occurrence. Butch turned and cried all the way to his house where he told his mother that Harvey hit him again.

George and Eddie Brooks

When George and Eddie Brooks enrolled at our school, it was one of the greatest days of my life. We didn't get many new kids, but these guys were very special to me. The last new student was a displaced kid from Greece who we taught our brand of English to as we played on the school's playground. In just a couple of months, he was speaking as poorly as the rest of us. But these guys were black, and that meant that I was no longer at the bottom of the social totem pole. Now, the Catholic boys had someone else to pick on for a change, and I couldn't have been more pleased. I made friends with the two brothers and would stick up for them whenever the boys from the St. Leo's school marched up the street looking for them. A couple of times, I led the two brothers down the pockmarked hill, but like the Catholics, they couldn't keep up with me. I would run back to the boys to help them, but by the time I got there, the gang of religious zealots had already surrounded the two brothers. Even bullies had their sense of fair play, so they decided to leave George alone since he was too small to kick around. But Eddie was another matter. It was my belief that all black guys, when backed into a corner, could fight like hell. After all, Joe Lewis was the best fighter in the world, and this kid even looked a little bit like the "Brown Bomber."

"C'mon Eddie, you can take him," I shouted. But my words fell on deaf ears because the poor guy was too scared to fight. Eddie didn't put up any resistance, and a minute later, he would start to cry. This ended any hope that he would beat the guy to a pulp. But in spite of his reluctance to fight the white guys, I remained friends with Eddie and George until the boys moved away a year later.

The Manolli Brothers

The Manolli brothers, Sammie and Joe, were sons of Italian immigrants who were burdened with having a drunk for a father. Joe, the older of the two brothers, would sometimes fight Snooky over reasons that were unclear. Perhaps it was because Joe just wanted to fight. He would start the raucous, then they would wrestle each other to the ground with Snooky ending up on top. After minute or two, Snooky who was winning at the time, would start to cry. Joe quickly reversed positions and got on top of my brother. "Come on, Snooky, you can beat him," everybody yelled. But he was finished and we all knew it. Snooky said, "uncle," and the fight was over. Once again, the Italian kid triumphed over my big brother.

On the other hand, his brother, Sammy, was a pal of mine. I would go to his decrepit wooden two story house that was badly in need of a paint job, to play in the parts of the backyard that hadn't been made into a vegetable garden by his dad. Late at night, I would hear Sammy or Joe walking their drunken father home from the bar. The youngsters urged their father, in Italian, to keep walking so that they could get him home and in bed. A few years later, their dad sobered up and things looked much brighter for the Manolli family. Their father finally painted their house, and Mr. Manolli remained sober for the rest of his life.

The Pleasant Surprise

When we learned that my mother was pregnant, it was a pleasant surprise for all of us. I hoped that it would be a girl because there were already three boys in the family, and that was more than enough for me. Finally, the day came for Mother to go to the hospital. When she delivered a beautiful baby girl, we were really excited to have a new member of our family. Although premature, she was healthy enough that after ten days, our new sister came home to join our family. My parents named her Janet Lynn, and both of my brothers and I were really happy to have her as our baby sister.

Driving The Neighborhood Nuts!

Inviting me into their house to play with Joe by Mrs. O'Connor, we had a pretty good time playing with his erector set and several of his other toys, but as he got a little older, while playing kick-the-can or some other kids' game in the back alley, Joe's mood would suddenly change, and he would turn into a Jew baiter. Donnie Shumaker would look at Snooky and me, then he would tell us that we'd better scram before O'Connor turned violent.

While Joe was in junior high school, his father built a barn up in the nearby woods. We could see the structure from our house where Mr. O'Connor kept a horse for his daughter to ride. Joe became a loner after he peed into a bottle of Coca Cola and gave it to a couple of the toughest guys in town, the O'Shea brothers. After tasting the wild concoction of coke and pee, the O'Shea boys were out to beat Joe to a pulp. From that day on, Joe chose to stay in his house and he never joined up with the gang again. As for the barn, Joe had the annoying habit of pounding on a steel barrel for several hours every day, and other than driving everybody in the neighborhood nuts, we had no idea why he was doing it. One day, my pal, Herbie Cohn, a Jewish kid who lived a block up the street, and I went up to the woods to play army. But what we saw, really upset us. Joe had taken to torturing the cats for a few days by putting them in a metal barrel and banging on the damn thing until they were driven insane by the pounding. After they were mesmerized, O'Conner picked them out of the barrel and hung them, like shirts on a clothesline, by their necks on the nearby tree branches.

Hebrew School

Four days a week, after the public schools dismissed for the day, the Jewish kids headed off to Hebrew School to learn the language of our ancestors and prepare for our Bar Mitzvahs. The classes was made up of mostly boys, who when we turned the magical age of thirteen, biblically became men. We didn't understand any of the words we were reading, but that didn't really matter. All we had to do was read the prayers with a degree of accuracy. As for me, my reading was as smooth as Betty Grable's skin on a Saturday night.

Normally, the rabbi would listen to the kids read, then correct us when we made mistakes. But our rabbi had a very dark side, and that wasn't a good thing. For reasons that I never figured out, he didn't seem to give a hoot about kids or anyone else for that matter. We heard that he had been a chaplain in the navy and, according to some of the guys, he had seen plenty of action in the Pacific. Perhaps those experiences had exposed the rabbi to the trauma of combat fatigue, but nevertheless, he was a cruel fellow. To add to the mysterious ways of our rabbi, we also believed that he kept a pistol in his desk. No one ever saw the gun, but the rumors persisted. One day, the rabbi was in a particularly foul mood and he decided to insult our parents, mine in particular. After deriding them, and me, my cousin Butch couldn't stand it any longer. He stood up and began to criticize the rabbi for making his nasty comments. Butch's display of poor judgment brought the rabbi's wrath down on him and he quickly forgot about me. My philosophy was that Jews survive by being discreet in moments of adversity. My poor cousin became a victim of the rabbi's anger because he didn't have any such philosophy. After class, Butch whined that I hadn't said anything while he was being cursed out. He was absolutely right about that! Another fight was in the cards, but the outcome was no different from all the other times.

The rabbi appeared to derive great pleasure out of insulting his daughter, Sandra, in front of the rest of the class. For example, if she asked to go to the bathroom, he'd say, "don't forget to wipe yourself." We felt sorry for poor Sandra and wished things could have been different between the two of them. She seldom talked to anyone, so we really didn't get to know her very well. Sandra and I went to the same junior high school, and it became a daily routine for me to wait for her to enter the school where the bullies would taunt her and overlook me. In other words, she ran interference for me by taking all the anti-Semitic remarks while I took the cowards way out by discreetly rushing passed them.

Through the falling snow and icy sidewalks, a class made their way from the Polish school to our synagogue for a field trip. When I heard they had come into the building, I asked the rabbi if I could go to the bathroom. As I walked out into the hallway, I saw about thirty boys and girls, and a nun, wrapped up in winter coats, warm hats, and babushkas. Covering their extremities were a collection of gloves and galoshes. Once again, I had revenge in mind for those damn Polish kids.

"Hello, Sister. If you want me to show you and the kids around the synagogue, I'd be happy to do so." I said, not unlike the spider to the fly. A bit of *schadenfreude,* if you will.

"Why yes. That would be very nice," answered the nun.

The smelly bathroom in the synagogue was totally disgusting. The old Jews from Europe were orthodox, and they didn't believe in flushing the toilets on the sabbath, or any other day for that matter. Thusly, the bathroom smelled like a Warsaw sewer. I also knew that the Poles believed that the devil smelled exactly like our bathroom.

"Do you want to see the Rabbi's office," I asked.

"Yes, that would be nice," answered the nun.

The Poles moved toward the bathroom door. "Let's all gather right here in front of the rabbi's door so that I can show you his office," I politely requested.

I opened the door to the bathroom part of the way so that the students couldn't see into the room, but they sure could get a whiff of the place. The kids, who just a moment ago had been an orderly group of students interested in seeing the rabbi's office, were now a frightened mob of howling maniacs. They shouted something in Polish, then the Sister and her once-subdued students fled from the synagogue screaming and crying.

Revenge was sweet. Grinning from ear to ear, I went back to class with a story to tell to my classmates after Hebrew School was over for the day.

My Bar Mitzvah lessons were going well, and the cantor was pleased with my steady progress. Cantor Leibowitz was a very gentle man who seemed to like me, and I was fond of the old guy from Europe who sang all the prayers at the services. By the time my Bar Mitzvah rolled around, I was well prepared to read the Torah and give an inspiring speech. Everything went well, and my parents were very proud of their Bar Mitzvah boy. Later that day, our house was loaded with food, and more importantly, tons of presents. I showed my brothers, and cousins, Francie and Butch, the gifts that were so numerous that they had to be stacked on my bed and against the wall of my bedroom. It was a great day, and like most Jewish boys, it was one that I'll always remember.

A year later, the rabbi and his family moved to New York where he apparently continued to treat Sandra in the same nasty way as he did in Altoona. It was in the big city that she passed away while still in her teens. When I learned of her tragic death, I think I know what killed her. It was a broken heart.

D.S. Keith Junior High School

Everything was full of promise on my first day at Keith Junior High School. I had purchased my Keith tee shirt, the one that I would wear in my physical education class, and at least for the moment, I had a new attitude about school. Now a junior high student, I no longer had to worry about the kids from St. Leo's or whether or not I was going to be a patrol boy. With new teachers and students, it had to be an improvement over Garfield Elementary School.

I had just finished talking to my big brother and his friend when things took a sudden turn for the worse. Failing to see the pile of fresh poop that some dog with diarrhea deposited on the school's sidewalk, I stepped on it. After trying desperately to separate my new Tom Brown shoes from the crap that was on them, I headed into the school to find my homeroom. Miss Loomer was my homeroom teacher, and after searching the third floor for a few moments, I found her room and quickly took my seat. That is when I noticed the two tough looking boys sitting beside me. And for some reason, they were laughing at me.

"Looks like we have a Jew boy sitting next to us," one of the ruffians said.

The other guy agreed, "Yeah. We got ourselves a Jew boy, all right."

At the time, I had no way of knowing that for the next two years I was going to be constantly harassed by those two cretins. Since no one would bother to listen anyway, not saying anything seemed to be my only option. Those two guys weren't the only anti-Semites in the school, but they certainly were the worst of the lot.

While in the eighth grade, my dad had one of Uncle Sam's saxophones that had been stored in our downstairs closet for a number of years, reconditioned. It was a C melody saxophone, but a few months later, he had the alto saxophone fixed as well. I joined the junior band

25

and practiced for several hours everyday, and all day on Saturdays and Sundays. Joe O'Connor, the future cat killer would shout from the street, "shut up, already!" But mother told me to ignore his insults and keep on playing. It wasn't long before I moved up the line of saxophonists to the first chair position. By the end of the year, the band director promoted me to the senior band. My success with music did a great deal for my ego, and I began feeling pretty good about myself. As an added bonus, the boys who once harassed me at the front door of the school were now friends. The exception was those two thugs who had been harassing me since the first day at Keith Junior High School, and they continued to taunt me until the day the boys picked on my friend, Frank Gross.

"Hey Gross, why doncha' quit talking to that guy? He's a Jew, you know. Maybe you're a Jew lover."

The other tough looking guy said, "Yeah. You're a Jew lover all right."

In the darkest recesses of my soul, I had stored up two years of hate for those creeps, and now it was time that I did something about it. Our student teacher had been called to the main office leaving the class unsupervised for at least ten minutes, so this was a good time to get back at them.

Getting up from my desk, I said in a loud voice, "Okay, that's it! I'm gonna' fight you two idiots right now. C'mon, let's go to the back of the room and get on with it."

Looking pretty cocky as they walked to the back of the class, both thugs laughed and goofed around just enough to make it seem like they were going to clean my clock. "We are going to get ourselves a Jew today," the rough looking guy said.

I waited just long enough for the meanest of the two guys to put up his dukes, then I plowed into him and began pounding the hell out of the fool. It really felt good, even therapeutic as my fists smashed into his ugly face. When I was finished with him, he was crying and whimpering. The class, who had witnessed the whole thing, were left in awe of my fighting prowess. Then I turned to the other stooge, "Now it's your turn. C'mon, let's go."

The second creep wanted no part of me. "Don't hit me. I don't want to fight you," he pleaded.

The poor slob was afraid of me, and at last, I realized that bullies were afraid of those they bullied. From that moment on and until we graduated from high school, I bugged those guys about their poor deportment and bad grades.

During my junior high school years, a very pretty girl named Susan Wright was my first crush. Her long brown hair, creamy complexion, eyes that sparkled like emeralds, a cute nose that pointed upward, and a shape that put an hour glass to shame, made her a really special girl. Susan lived in the Third Ward just three blocks, as the crow flies, over the hill from my house. At night, I would lie in my bed and look out the window wondering if she could see the same street lamp that lit up the hill separating her neighborhood from mine. Every morning, depending on the season, her dad would either be tending to the flowers in his front garden, or shoveling the snow by the time I got to her house. Mr. Wright would smile and greet me the same way every morning.

"Good morning, son. She'll be out in just a minute." He didn't seem to have a prejudiced bone in his body.

Everyday, Susan and I trekked up the steep hill to school, and whenever I had an empty hand, she would let me carry her books. After school was out, we would wait for each other then walk back down the hill where would talk about school and how things were going with the band.

I never asked her out on a date, but all my classmates at Keith Junior High School thought that we were special friends, and that was swell by me.

Miss England, our ninth grade English teacher, was a pretty redhead who was endowed with a young and slender frame. Larry Gannett, the school's thespian, and I had a crush on the pretty teacher. The two of us would stop by her room after school for a quick chat and a laugh or two. After she assigned us to learn the Lincoln's Gettysburg Address, each member of the class was required to stand up and recite it. Larry and I had agreed that we would flub up on the recitation and act like we hadn't memorized it. Well, as anticipated, both Larry and I had to remain after school until we were able to recite the Gettysburg Address. On Monday, Tuesday, and Wednesday, we goofed around and pretended to be unable to recite it. Finally, on Thursday, she caught on to our trick. That was when she made us stand up and recite "Four score and seven years ago, our forefathers...

At Keith Junior High School, I had a couple of close friends, Jake Dellinger, who was Jewish, and Ronnie O'Brian, a handsome Irish kid who was very popular with the girls. Both were incredible musicians. Ronnie played the trombone, and his tone was as sweet as cotton candy at the country fair. Jake played tuba and bass fiddle, and if it were written, he could play it.

School was out for the day when Mr. Black, a history teacher at Keith Junior High School, whose son later became my college roommate, drove past us on his way home. Without thinking, Ronnie said, "There is Mr. Black, that dirty Jew." Alarmed by his own prejudice, he immediately realized what he said, and quickly apologized.

"I'm sorry, Harv. I didn't mean it," he said. Never again did I hear any remarks about Jews from Ronnie O'Brian trombone playing lips.

Altoona High School

My brother, Lou, put together a dance band and we got our first job at a former fire station that was located just across the street from Garfield Elementary School. Loud and lousy best described our sound, but with each performance, we improved. My dad supported our musical endeavors by driving us to our performances, then he stayed with us as we played *Blue Moon, Once In A While, Over The Rainbow,* and a bunch of other standards. Afterwards, dad would help us pack up before driving Ronnie O'Brian, Jackie McCord, Joey Hunter, and Jake Dellinger back to their homes. Our theme was *Moonlight Serenade,* and the name of our band was "Lou Getz and his Melody Men."

While in the second semester of the tenth grade, my girlfriend at the time, Sandy McBride, was Irish. This meant that I couldn't go into their house, yet alone date Sandy. But on Saturday nights, Ronnie O'Brian would go to Sandy's house under the guise that he was the fellow that she was going out with. After the two of them left her place, they climbed into the back seat of my car until we drove around the next corner. Once out of sight, we'd switch dates, kiss a couple of times, then we were off to the movies. We continued this routine for about three months, then she dumped me for Zane Williamson, our high school band's drum major.

After Jake's father died unexpectedly of a heart attack, I became pals with Jake Dellinger. To help him cope with his father's death, I'd ride my bike out to Jake's house nearly every day to spend time playing, or just sitting around chewing the fat. We soon became best friends, and we remained that way until after he graduated from Indiana State College in Pennsylvania. While in high school, when we weren't playing in the Lou Getz and His Melody Men band, we'd go to Dave's Dream for some coke, cheeseburgers and fries. Afterwards, Jake drove me back to my house where we would sit in his car and talk for hours about what the future held for us, and of course, girls.

Following an away football game, because the guys from Johnstown were only a half a step up from being Neanderthals, a riot broke out when they had lost the game between our two rival schools. In Altoona High School band uniforms, we were an easy prey for the angry mob of Johnstowners.

Running back to the bus as fast as our musical instruments would allow, a flag girl, Nancy Tylenis, caught up with me and asked for help getting back to the bus. I yelled, "You should ask Jake Dellinger, he's a lot bigger than me." Jake was over six feet tall, and built like a line backer, but I grabbed her hand and headed straight for the safety of the bus. Once there, we quickly found two seats together.

As the boys and girls retreated into the band bus, it was the first and last time I ever heard our band director swear. "Lets get the hell of here," Mr. Mariano yelled to the panic-stricken driver.

Quickly exiting the football field, we sped over the mountains for the forty-mile trip back to Altoona. Nancy and I huddled together in the cold bus and held hands under the blanket that she had brought with her.

After arriving back at the high school, Nancy asked me if I would walk her home. Since she also lived in the Fifth Ward, somewhere near Garfield School, I was more than happy to do so. We stomped through the snow-covered streets, headed across the Twelfth Street railroad bridge, then up the steep and icy Fourteenth Avenue hill. It was the same hill where I made bets with my cousin, Butch, whether or not the old Jews coming from the synagogue would make it all the way up the icy sidewalk without falling back down the hill. Finally, we made it to the top of the incline, then we walked past Garfield Elementary School. Clear and cold, the fresh night air felt refreshing and invigorating. When we arrived on the front porch of her two-story wooden house, Nancy and I looked up at the full moon shining through the snowflakes, and our lips delightfully collided.

Her father, who slept with his bedroom window open even in the winter, suddenly interrupted us.

"Nancy. Is that you?" I think he was speaking Lithuanian.

She whispered to me that she was going to speak Lithuanian. "Yes, father. It's me."

Both of us looked up at the winter sky, and once again, and we got in another sweet kiss or two until her father broke the silence that a kiss makes.

"Are you alone," he shouted.

"No, father. I am not alone."

Another minute passed before he spoke again, "What is his name?"

"You don't know him. But it's all right. He is Lithuanian."

After that, there were no more interruptions.

Being Lithuanian wasn't really a part of of my soul, but there was one other time when it certainly had its advantages. When not playing in my brother's band, I'd get telephone calls from Joe Grinius, a trumpet player, to sit in with his Polish band to play in some pretty rough places up in the coal mining towns of Pennsylvania. One joint had some real tough characters, and when the coal miners were stinking drunk, they would terrorize the place. That particular club had a wired and locked cage where the bands played their polkas and mazurkas. When asked by the proprietor if we wanted to take a break, we chorused, "No thanks. We'll just stay in the cage."

Back in those days, going into another guy's house was a pretty big deal. A fellow didn't enter a house unless his mother said it was all right to do so. Joe Grinius, and his brother, Mike, lived two blocks away on Nineteen Street. Joe would phone me to come pick up the music for the Saturday night gigs and I would run two blocks over to their place to meet them on the sidewalk in front of their house. After a few times talking on the sidewalk, Joe invited me up onto the porch to discuss the tunes and what time they would pick me up. A couple of weeks later, while discussing our next job, Joe said to me, "My mother would like to meet you. She told me that she would like to meet you today."

I replied, "Certainly. I'd like to meet your mother, too."

"Mom, come out here and meet Harvey," Mike yelled into the house. His voice showed a great deal of respect in spite of the volume of his request.

Like a blossoming flower, their mother appeared on the front porch. She was a very attractive and petite woman who moved with the grace of a ballerina. Her blond hair was wrapped in a string of tied up pigtails making her look very European. She smiled pleasantly, "It is a pleasure to meet you, Harvey. I've been hearing nice things about you."

"Thank you, ma'am. It's very nice to meet you, Mrs. Grinius," I said.

Mike and Joe's mother had a smile that could instantly melt a gallon of Sealtest ice cream.

"Please tell me. Where are you from?" she asked.

"Over on Eighteen Street. Just a couple of blocks from here," I replied.

She took her index finger and waved it from side to side. "No. I mean where are you FROM?"

"Oh, you mean...uh..Lithuania," I replied.

She laughed, "We are from Lithuania, too. And you can come into the house."

John Mariano

Our high school band director, Mr. John C. Mariano, was an Italian-American who was born in Catania, Sicily. He arrived in America at a very young age, and later in his life, he became the conductor of the Altoona High School band. It was a esteemed position making Mr. Mariano a town celebrity of sorts. In his marching band, there were 145 members, all of whom were boys. The girls were allowed to play in the concert band, but the marching band was strictly a male dominated ensemble. It wouldn't go over that way in today's world, but back on those days, it was simply the way things were done. Yes, there were girls twirling batons and carrying flags, but they were incidental to the sound that came from the band. When we marched up Eleven Avenue with trombones roaring, trumpets blasting away, drums pounding, and saxophones, flutes and clarinets doing their very best to be heard, it was an astounding experience for both the band members and their audiences. Marching on the right side of the band, he was full of pride for the musical organization that he so passionately loved. In short, we were nothing less than terrific.

Lou Getz and his Melody Men were growing increasing popular, but to Mr. Mariano, we were "scabs." As non-union members, we took jobs away from the struggling union musicians. In the eyes of Mr. Mariano, this equated to making us thieves who stole bread from the musicians' kitchen tables. Whenever he had the chance, he would point this out and treat us like food thieves instead of musicians. During the second semester of my sophomore year, Mr. Mariano called my dad and asked if he could take us to the musicians union meeting at the Penn Alto Hotel to become union members. My dad quickly agreed. On Thursday evening, he drove us to the meeting where we became card-carrying members of the musicians union. Our status in the high school band immediately improved, and during my junior year, I took over first chair and played solos in the next two annual concerts. To this day, whenever I don't practice my saxophone for a while, Mr. Mariano appears in a dream and tells me to get back to my horn.

Bob McKibben was a fellow who played third clarinet in the last chair of the large section of clarinets. The placement of both he and his horn was convenient as far as Mr. Mariano was concerned. Bob had the habit of getting kicked out of band class on a regular basis, so his position close to the door made it a simple matter of convenient geography. One day, he came to band late for class. When Mr. Mariano asked him what the problem was, he replied, "You are lucky that I'm here."

Mr. Mariano got a look of indifference on his face then he yelled, "McKibben. Get out, now!"

Once again, Bob was free to roam the halls of Altoona High School. After his graduation, he joined the Army and rode around in tanks with the 3rd Armored Division in Germany. A few years later, when he got out of the service, he gave me one of his fatigue shirts and his zippered paratrooper boots. I wore them as part of my National Guard uniform.

The Girl In The Green Plaid Swimming Suit

It was a Friday afternoon, during the summer of our junior year, when Jake Dellinger and I went out to the Lakemont Park to swim and gaze at the girls lounging around in the grass-covered area adjacent to the pool.

"Wow! Look at that girl sitting over there!" I exclaimed. Sitting on her blanket was the most incredible girl that my sixteen year old eyes had ever seen.

"You mean the one with the blue bathing suit?" Jake asked.

"No. I mean the girl wearing the green plaid bathing suit."

"Oh yeah, she's a really good-looking girl, all right. What do say we go over and talk to them?"

A few minutes later, we were chatting with the two girls from Hollidaysburg, Barbara Monroe and Janine Michaels. Barbara, a red-haired beauty, was the girl that I was interested in getting to know better. Both girls were in their high school band, so the four of us talked about music until it was time for them to leave. For the next couple of days, I couldn't forget the girl whose eyes sparkled like blue sapphires, had a smile that could warm the coldest of hearts, and her voice was as soft and sweet as a fresh piece of watermelon.

It took me until Wednesday to finally get up enough courage to telephone Barbara for a date. My hand was shaking as I dialed up her number and her mother answered the phone. I asked her if I could please speak with Barbara. A minute later, she came to the phone, and after a bit of small talk, I swallowed hard and asked her to go the movies.

She thought about it for a moment, then asked, "Well, all right. What time will you pick me up?"

Now very excited about going out with Barbara, I did my best to stay calm, cool, and collected.

"Is six-thirty all right with you?" I inquired.

"Yes, that will be fine," she answered.

To look my best for my date with Barbara, I went to my barbershop for a haircut. The two brothers from Sicily, who competed with operatic tunes on their record player, operated the shop. Carefully placed on the shelf in front of the mirror next to the lotions and creams, was a portable record player, and while giving me a haircut, they played their music and explained the stories of the various operas. In turn, I would ask questions about the operas such as, "Why did Madam Chio Chio kill herself instead of waiting for Lt. Pinkerton to return?" Or, in the opera Barbiere di Sivigla, "If Almaviva was so clever, why didn't he just elope with the beautiful Rosina in the first place?"

"Do you have a date this weekend?" Joe asked.

"Yes, I do." I replied.

"Clip, clip, clip. Is she a nice girl?" Joe inquired.

"A very nice girl," I said.

Antonio asked, "Do you know how to tell whether a girl really likes you or not?"

"Clip, clip, clip." I answered, "No, I don't. But please tell me."

Antonio answered, "When you open the door to let her in the car, if she reaches over to unlock your door for you, that's when you know that she likes you."

I gave a hearty laugh, but I would try it on my first date with Barbara Ann Monroe.

Saturday finally arrived and I tried the barber's trick. And I'll be darned if it didn't work. She reached her arm over to unlock the door and that was the moment that I knew she liked me.

That small gesture was the beginning of a wonderful romance that lasted for more than two years. During that time, we had a routine of sorts. On Friday nights, we went to the YWCA, just a couple of blocks up the street from her house. On those cold winter nights, after a night of dancing, the walk back to Barbara's place was somewhere between fantastic and magical. Penn Street, with its blanket of snow covering the road and the overhanging trees, was both breathtaking and picturesque. It looked like a page out of a children's winter fairy tale book. Barbara's red hair had the fresh smell of falling snow, and her slender body emitted a slight lavender aroma as we walked hand-in-hand back to her house.

On Saturday nights, we went to the movies in Altoona, followed by a cheeseburger and a coke at Taylor's Drive Inn. From time to time, I would drive out to her house during the week to get some help with my math homework. Those tutoring sessions resulted in my going from an average to an honor roll student in record time. I figured that Barbara didn't want any dummies around, so I really started to apply myself in school. Things continued to go well for us until her father found out I was Jewish. After that, Mr. Monroe didn't talk to me anymore.

Jack Colbert was also a Hollidaysburg High School student who played lead trumpet in their high school band. He had asked Barbara to go out with him on several occasions, although she turned him down, I certainly felt some hostility toward the guy.

One hot summer evening, I went to Lakemont Park to listen to the union band play at the dance pavilion, and maybe even get in a dance or two. At the dance hall was the guy I disliked, Jack Colbert. It was ladies choice, but for some odd reason neither of us was chosen. And that is when I walked over to Jack and remarked, "Looks like both of us are sitting this one out."

He laughed, "Yeah, I guess this isn't our night. In spite of not liking the guy, it was a good laugh. A couple of minutes later he said, "C'mon Harv. What do you say we get out of here and go for a couple of beers?"

At first I was surprised by his suggestion, but I figured it couldn't hurt anything, so I said, "All right. I might know just the place to have a few brews."

At a bar in Altoona, that neither of us had been to before, we became friends. After drinking heavily for a couple of hours, I decided that it was best if he slept it off at my house. Jack lived out in Duncansville, a town of about 500 people, about six miles on the Hollidaysburg side of Altoona; too far for the inebriated young man to drive home. So that night, we slept in my bed. The next morning, we both had slight hangovers, but we were as hungry as a pair of starving wolves. After getting out of bed, I introduced him to my mother. She greeted us cheerfully, then she went downstairs and got busy making pancakes and eggs for us. What a good woman! There were several more occasions over the next couple of years when Jack slept it off at my house.

Barbara and I continued to see each other, but shortly after becoming a freshman at Penn State, she ditched me for an even luckier fellow.

Shippensburg State Teachers College

After graduating from Altoona High School, I had no idea what the future might hold for me. I hadn't made any plans for college, but in early July, my brother said that I might still have a chance to go his school.

"We are going to Shippensburg State. They are giving the last entrance test this Saturday. And guess what? You are going to take it."

Come to think of it, going to Shippensburg wasn't such a bad idea. It would at least give me something to do with my time, and who knows, I might even like the place.

We drove over the mountains the following Saturday to Shippensburg State College to take the entrance test. After a couple hours of driving, we arrived on campus where my brother pointed out the auditorium before he went to a nearby restaurant for some breakfast. After I took a seat in the fairly new building, the proctors passed out writing pads and pencils to each of the aspiring candidates. The fellow administering the test said, "There will only be fifty of you that will make it to the freshmen class, and those will be the top fifty scores."

I looked around the auditorium and estimated that approximately 150 men and women were taking the test. I said to myself, *fat chance I have to pass this thing, but I'll give it the old college try.*

After I finished the exam, we drove back over the mountains to Altoona without my having the slightest clue whether I passed it or not. A week later, a letter from Shippensburg State College arrived in our mailbox. I slowly opened the letter fully expecting it to be a rejection notice. Instead, I had passed the test and was on my way to becoming a member of the freshman class of 1956.

The Campus Fountain

Next to the campus fountain, several upperclassmen were getting their thrills by holding a rally of sorts. Believing it was their duty to think up ways to punish the hapless freshmen, they were a particularly obnoxious lot. I was in the National Guard and I didn't feel like taking any crap from those guys. I was thinking about this when one of the boys ordered me to get into the fountain.

"I'm not getting into the water. It will ruin my new saddle shoes and clothes," I protested.

"Get into the water," repeated the upperclassman. This time, he had a threatening tone to his voice.

"I'm not getting into that water. Like I said, I don't want to ruin my shoes and my clothes."

By this time, a crowd of students gathered to watch him throw me into the fountain. When he grabbed me to toss me in, I got a grip on the guy and applied a hip throw and promptly deposited the poor fellow into the water. A minute later, a mob of upper classroom gave chase, but just like the Catholic boys who hobbled down that ditch-filled hill years ago, I outran them. I sped up a couple flights of stairs and into my room, then I quickly locked the door. They tried like hell to get in, but they couldn't break down the heavy oak door. A couple of guys tried climbing through the window, but I rushed over and locked it. Now, there was no way they could get into the room. As a precaution, I remained inside for the rest of the night before venturing back outside the next morning. By then, all but the guy I'd thrown in the fountain had forgotten about it.

A Farewell To Shippensburg State Teachers College

The fall leaves were changing color and slowly plummeting to the earth, and so was my reputation with a couple of professors at Shippensburg State Teachers College. The first of the two episodes occurred in my English class. During one of his daily lectures, I incurred the wrath of my English professor by proving that he was wrong about our first president, George Washington. Charles Fellows declared that George Washington, according to the professor's definition, was a true gentleman.

"He always did the right thing socially, and he came from a long line of gentlemen," was the teacher's simplified definition.

Being the poor slob who asked Dr. Fellows about George Washington, I pointed out that the general had contacted a socially transmitted disease from an island maiden. I thought that under Dr. Fellows' definition, this disqualified him from being a gentleman. My opposing bit of information caused the professor to go ballistic. After that revelation, I was nothing but chopped liver in his class.

My American history professor believed that a freshman sitting in a class for juniors should receive nothing higher than a "C" grade. On every test, I didn't make any mistakes, but I continued to get "C's." American history was my favorite subject and I expected my grades to be much higher. Some of the fellows in the class, who were juniors, copied from my paper when the teacher was out of the room, and most of them ended up with "A's" on their exams. I made an appointment with Professor Fox to clarify the matter, but he ignored my argument. Instead he replied, "You are a freshman. The best you can hope for is a 'C' no matter how well you do in the class discussion or on the exams."

The final blow at Shippensburg State College came when my brother and I double dated to a distant college hangout filled with students from the Naval Academy, Hagerstown, Dickinson, Gettysburg, and a few other schools. Once we got to the nightclub, my date started to guzzle down drink after drink until she was drunk as a skunk. In fact, I had to hold her up while we were dancing or she would have fallen flat on her face. Embarrassed, I gave up and sat down until we were ready to leave the dance hall. In the car, she cuddled up against me, but I was disgusted with her, so I didn't touch her. Throughout the entire drive back to the campus, my brother and his date were no more than two feet away from us, so if I were going to try something, I would have had to do it in front of them. When she got back to her dorm, I said a quick good night and then headed back to the men's dorm. The next day, for some strange reason, all of the girls on campus were giving me the silent treatment. Naturally, I wanted to know why I was being given the cold shoulder. When I asked Fred Klein, who knew all the things a guy wanted to know about life at Shippensburg State replied, "I don't know, but I'll find out and let you know."

When I learned what she had said, I was angry and disgusted. She reported to her girlfriends that I tried to rape her. That is when I went to the Dean of Men to tell him that the allegations were totally false.

"Dr. Smaltz, I would never do such a thing. It's against everything I stand for."

"Yes, I know that, Harvey. I realize that it is a complete fabrication. Tell me, Harvey, does this school seem too small for you?"

"I guess the place does seem kind of small. I tried to get a few debates going in my classes, but that didn't go over very well. I thought that was what college was about," I said.

Pausing to light his pipe, and after taking a couple of drags, he said, "Yes, I'm afraid that sort of thing doesn't go off very well here at Shippensburg. You know, Harvey, you tested very high on the entrance exam. Have you thought about going to another school? A larger school?"

"Yes, I have been thinking about it," I said.

"Where would you like to go?" He asked.

I gave it some thought before replying, "Penn State University."

"All right," he answered. "Get your grades up, and I'll get you into Penn State next semester."

Dr. Smaltz didn't have to help me, but he gave me the break of my young life. I figured that I would someday like to do the same for my students. And that is how one good turn from the Dean of Men influenced me throughout my long career in education.

Summer Vacation

Summer vacation was a great time mainly because it gave me the freedom to do the things that I wasn't able to do during the school year. During those short but sweet breaks, I was free to hit the bars around Altoona with my friends, and sleep late when I felt like it.

Finding myself thirsty for a cold beer, I drove out to a bar on the outskirts of Altoona to enjoy a brew or two. While I was into my first sip, an old acquaintance from my Garfield days came into the club with her skinny, but indignant boyfriend. Apparently, she had told him horror stories about the school, and one of them was the way the boys at Garfield School mistreated her. During our elementary school days, she was very poor, and this made her an easy target for the guys to tease her about her clothes and soiled face. As Cindy got older, she was able to find a job and buy some nice clothes and makeup, but it was obvious that she hadn't forgotten about her school days, and her boyfriend was determined to avenge every wrong that had happened to her.

"Hello, Cindy. It has been a long time since I've seen you," I said.

At that point, her boyfriend headed in my direction, and from the look on his face and his clenched fists, he was prepared to fight me. "Oh no. Not him!" she shouted. "He was always very nice to me."

He stopped dead in his tracks and retreated back to his girlfriend.

Ignoring him, I said, "It's nice seeing you again, Cindy. How have you been?"

She answered, "Fine, thank you. It's good to see you again, too."

If I hadn't treated Cindy with dignity when I was an elementary school student, I would have found myself in a fight with her knight in shining armour.

I got a job that summer selling leather bound white bibles with everything the good lord Jesus said was printed in red. And if they bought a bible, they were given a beautiful gypsy red rose lamp. Unfortunately, it was my fate not to sell any bibles for the simple reason that the out-of-work and mostly sick miners were too poor to buy them. But they sure liked the bible and the lamp when I showed them the lighted base with the painted red rose.

Wildwood, New Jersey

Jack Colbert, Jake Dellinger and I, during the summer of our junior year, joined a couple of other fellows for an adventure in Wildwood, New Jersey. My first job was at an Italian restaurant owned by a Sicilian who looked at Jake Dellinger and I and immediately saw a couple of meatball makers. After teaching us how to roll the meatballs, he left us alone to keep the kitchen clean and prepare the meatballs before placing them into a boiling vat. After several days on the job, he grabbed two chairs and told us to sit there when we ran out of things to do. A few hours later, we had cleaned the already spotless kitchen for the fifth time and made another batch of meatballs. It was then that we both agreed that we had run out of things to do. So we sat down to rest in the two chairs the boss had provided for us. But no sooner had we placed our sweet asses into the seats when the owner came into the kitchen and saw us sitting there like a couple of crows on a dead oak tree.

"What the hell is this? I don't need a bunch of lazy bums sitting around doing nothing. Both you guys are fired. Now get the hell outta' here!"

It was at that moment that I saw the crazed look in Jake's eyes. It was the look of a guy about to toss several pounds of meatballs all over the man's kitchen.

"No, Jake," I cautioned, "the police in this town are pretty rough on college students. Let's just get the hell out of here."

I led Jake Dellinger to the kitchen door and safely out to the freedom of the street. It was goodbye to the idiot of an owner, and to his lousy meatballs. The owner apparently was a frugal fellow because he never did pay us for our week's work at the restaurant.

After a couple of hours on the job as a soda jerk, I got fired because I was too slow for the waitresses. There were about thirty different ice cream combinations, so I had to read the menus in order to find out what the ingredients were. As far as the waitresses were concerned, this method slowed them down as they tried to provide quick service to their customers. Left without a job, Jack Colbert and I decided to return to Altoona to lick our wounds. As we sped down the Jersey turnpike in Jack's new Ford Fairlane, we decided to stop in Newark to visit with a stewardess friend of his for the night. Before going to her place, we went to a cafe and ordered a single bowl of Campbell's chicken noodle soup and crackers for two. Being short of funds, that is all we could afford, but the noodle soup sure tasted great. After we slowly finished slurping it down, we went to his friend's apartment. When we asked if we could stay for the night, the flight attendant reluctantly agreed. However, after getting comfortable on her couch, she came running back into the room and she told us that we had better leave at once because the owner was coming over to the apartment. We didn't believe her, but we had no choice but to hit the road.

It was about four o'clock in the morning when we found ourselves lost somewhere in the hills of upstate New York. The dashboard lights reflected the concern on Jack's face as we drove somewhere on the road to nowhere. We were on a back country road when we suddenly came upon a group of soldiers waving their arms and ordering us to stop.

"Christ, I think we are somewhere on the grounds at West Point," I said.

"What the hell! How did we get here?" Jack asked.

"I don't know, but you better let me handle this," I urged. "Being in the National Guard, I think I know how to handle these guys."

"Hello there." I knew it was best to speak first. "Man, are we really glad to see you guys. Where are we anyway? We are really lost," I said.

"You guys sure are in the wrong place at the wrong time." Even in the dark, I could see his smile.

"Yes, we sure are." I agreed.

"I'll tell you what you should do," he said. "Head back the way you were came for about two miles, then make the first left turn that you can. After a half of mile, you'll be on the main road."

"Thanks a lot, sergeant. We sure don't want to interfere with anything you fellows are doing."

"That's OK. Just clear the area," he added.

"Well, take care of yourself. And good luck," I said.

"You guys take care of yourselves, too," replied the army cadet.

In spite of the nearly empty gas tank, we made it back to Altoona. After getting to my house, we asked my mother to make us a couple of bowls of Campbell's noodle soup and lots of crackers.

Penn State University

Dave Black was a jack-of-all trades who could repair anything from motorcycles to grandfather clocks. If looks meant anything, he was one of the best-looking guys at Penn State. And if brawn was what you wanted, he was the middleweight golden glove champion of Pennsylvania. In short, he was the man for all seasons. Dave, sporting a dark complexion, a beautiful head of black hair, and a body with muscles protruding in all the right places, looked more like a Greek god than a mere mortal.

He was majoring in mechanical engineering, and after we became roommates, it didn't take long for me to mirror some of his study habits. Until it was time for the semester exams, he didn't do a hell of a lot of studying. Black tried to get a semester's work under his belt with all night study sessions that included a couple of cigars and some Nodoz pills to keep him awake. But he had his fine points as well. When we needed a few extra bucks to see us through until the end of the month, Dave went to Bellefonte, Pennsylvania to hustle money from table tennis and unsuspecting pool players. At the student union, Dave managed to gather a small group of loyal friends who sat around shooting the bull, while class attendance was a casual affair for most of us.

Sunshine, rain, or snow, we'd ride on his Harley-Davidson motorcycle to Altoona and around the campus wearing large rubber noses and fake glasses. Keeping warm was a priority during those long and cold Pennsylvania winter months, that is why we both wore fur-lined US Air Force Alaskan parkas while traveling around on his motorcycle.

A Trumpet Player

Trumpet great, John Yardley, who had just got out of the slammer for using drugs, was back in Altoona to get his chops back. A jazz group from Philadelphia was coming to State College, and Yardley planned to sit in with the group. He and his wife came up to Penn State, and I invited them to stay at our place for the night. John and I played in the union band together, and that is where I got to know the famous jazz musician. Dave and I went over to a fraternity house for the night, so the apartment was available to them. That evening, John and I walked over to the jazz club where he planned to sit in with the band. But after we got there, the leader of the group stubbornly refused to let him play. Here was a trumpet player who played and recorded with the likes of Gerry Mulligan, Zoot Sims, Teddy Kotick, Bob Brookmeyer, and Phil Woods, and he was literally begging to sit in with a group of unknowns. That night, he didn't get to play his horn, but while staying at my place, he wrote a song for me and left it on my desk. He titled it, "Theme For Harvey." Much to the chagrin of my roommate, John and his wife also left several empty bottles of codeine lying around on the floor.

The Residential Hoax

The weekend before spring break, I brought our second car from home and left it parked in front of our apartment for the week. One of the girls that I dated was a Jewish girl with a great personality who also happened to be pretty cute. She had pretty brown eyes and skin as smooth as a peach, and a slim body. Feeling really great about the pending vacation, and it wasn't too far out of the way, I offered to give Donna Segal a ride to her home in Johnstown, just forty miles over the mountains from Altoona. During the trip, we chatted and were having a nice time as we drove through Tyrone then onto Plank Road. When we were on the outskirts of Altoona, I told her that I had to stop by my house to tell my parents that I would be late for dinner. As I rounded the corner in the wealthy part of town, we came upon an old antebellum mansion that was once the home of the Blair family, but it had been converted in the county museum. Donna didn't know that, so I casually mentioned that I lived there. Donna's jaw dropped an inch or two as she stared at the palatial mansion.

"Please wait here while I tell Charles that I will be late getting home tonight."

I walked over to the fellow who was a well-dressed employee wearing a tuxedo, "Pardon me, sir. What hours are you open?

The guard replied, "From 10:00 till 4:00 PM."

I walked back to the car and told her, "Charles said that he would tell my parents that I was going to be late."

After the spring break, Donna Segal couldn't wait to tell all of her friends about the Getz mansion in Altoona.

Two Girls From Shippensburg State

One dark and snowy night, Dave paced back and forth trying to wear out the tiles on the floor of our one-room apartment. Finally, breaking his silence, he said, "Harv, I want to meet someone new. I want to meet a girl who can excite me. If you know what I mean."

"Well, I don't know if I can help you with that," I replied,

"Maybe if we get off campus and go somewhere," he said.

I thought about it for a minute. Suddenly, I remembered a couple of girls at Shippensburg State College who might meet his needs.

"I think I have an idea," I said.

Dave challenged, "Come on, Harv. Out with it!"

"Well, there are a couple of girls at Shippensburg that you might find interesting," I replied.

Now excited by the prospect of meeting someone new, he said, "Let's go. We'll grab our toothbrushes and get the hell out of here."

"You mean now? C'mon Dave, it's in the middle of the night, and it is snowing like hell out there," I protested.

"My trustee Studebaker will take us anywhere at anytime," he bragged.

So we got our toothbrushes, wiped the snow off the car, then we were off over the mountains to Shippensburg. Traveling through the night, the sunlight finally broke through the darkness as we approached a curve that I remembered as quite treacherous.

I warned Dave, "We are coming up to a very sharp curve, so I think you had better slow down.

He replied, "Don't sweat it. This car can make any curve."

"I'm telling you. We are not going to make it. Slow down, please. It's really dangerous," I pleaded.

When we hit the curve, and Dave was completely surprised by its severity. He turned the bullet shaped vehicle to the left, then to the right, but it didn't do any good. The turn was so sharp that we slid off the side of the road and plowed into a snow bank. Both the bullet nosed car and its passengers were completely buried in the white stuff.

"I hate to tell you this, but I told you so," I moaned.

"Jesus! That was a really sharp curve," was all he could say.

It took us about 30 minutes to dig our way out of our snowy grave and free the car. Finally, we were back on the road to Shippensburg. And other than the driver's bruised ego, there was no damage done to his precious Studebaker.

About forty minutes later, we arrived on the Shippensburg campus. We asked several people where Helen and Jean lived, but they didn't know, but a short time later, a former classmate of mine directed us to their house. It was only a couple of blocks from the campus.

I knocked on the door of their freshly painted wooden house, and a minute later, Jean answered the door. Her roommate, Helen, was standing directly behind her. The two girls, who were still in their pajamas, were surprised and very excited to see us. Since we dated a few times when I was at Shippensburg, Jean was with me, and Helen, who was thrilled to meet Dave, gladly paired up with him. After the greetings and introductions were over, they got dressed and we went to the town's favorite coffee shop for breakfast. The old restaurant hadn't changed a bit since the last time I was there. The booths were covered with the same red and white vinyl plastic, and Frank Sinatra was still crooning, *All The Way*, on the jukebox as we ordered four helpings of coffee, pancakes, and eggs.

That evening, Jean and I went to the movie theatre to see, "In Love In War," starring a couple of young guys named Robert Wagner and Jeffrey Hunter. They played courageous Marines fighting the bloody war in the Pacific. In the end, Wagner survived, and Hunter, who played a sergeant, didn't. Meanwhile, Dave and Helen were off somewhere doing their thing. After getting back together, Dave and I slept on the couch that night with pillows and blankets provided by Helen. The next morning, we went back to the restaurant. After eating a hearty breakfast, Dave and I said our goodbyes to the girls and promised to return soon. We headed back to Penn State, but on our return trip, this time, Dave respected the sharp curve.

After a few months of traveling to Shippensburg, Dave grew tired of Helen, and it was over for the two of them. As for Jean and I, although she had boyfriends and I had girlfriends, we continued to see each other. The next couple of years passed quickly, but Altoona's buses were as slow as ever. Growing tired of waiting for the Fifth Ward bus, Lou and I hopped on the Third Ward bus after deciding that a short walk over the hill was preferable to waiting. We entered the bus and were about to take our seats when I noticed that an old friend, Susan Wright, was also on the bus. And she was as good looking as ever. We sat down next to Susan, who told us that she was a junior at Slippery Rock State Teachers College where she was studying to be an elementary teacher. I told Susan that I was going to Penn State and also majoring in education. We talked all the way to our bus stop and when it was time to say goodbye, Lou and I wished her good luck, and I told her that it was great seeing her again. Unfortunately, it was the last time I ever saw the girl who had stolen my heart a few years earlier.

The Pennsylvania National Guard

As a soldier promoted to corporal, then busted back to a private first class for wearing black socks with a red thread at the very top of the footgear, my eight years in the Pennsylvania National Guard were remarkably undistinguished. On the other hand, as a member of the 28th Infantry Division Band, I was lucky to be among a group of fifty other musicians, who for the most part, were good friends, including my brothers, Lou and Allen, Jake Dellinger, and Ronnie O'Brian.

We went to the army training grounds at Indiantown Gap every summer to play soldiers for a couple of weeks. At the ungodly hour of 0430, the band would march over to the officers' quarters to sound reveille by playing, *And The Caissons Go Rollin' Along*. After returning to our barracks, we went to the chow hall with mess kits in hand and empty stomachs. Making a fairly decent breakfast, the cooks filled our kits with eggs, potatoes, bacon, and a couple of slices of toast, and all the coffee that we could drink. Once we finished eating, we would step outside to dip our tin ware in the barrel of scalding water, then walk back to our barracks to prepare for our daily inspections. The cleaning of the barracks was a very important task, as was the making up of our bunks. Everything had to be perfect. To ensure that the covers on our bunks were tight enough, we bounced quarters off of them, and if they didn't bounce back at you, they wouldn't pass inspection. Work details were formed, so we went about the business of scrubbing the floors, cleaning the windows, and polishing the latrine until the commodes, even in the dim light, sparkled. After a couple of summers of diligently working to keep the place clean, I learned to walk around the barracks with a rag in my hand and act as if I were really busy. Once we were finished with cleaning the barracks, we went outside and marched around in the morning sun for an hour. After we finished parading around the field, we followed up with our morning rehearsals, which usually lasted until lunchtime. In the afternoon, we continued to rehearse before preparing our uniforms for the evening retreat ceremony.

After the Pass-In-Review ceremony, the day came to a close and we had the rest of the evening to do whatever we wanted as long as we didn't piss off the military police. Most of us, after evening chow, would board a bus in our Class A uniforms and go either to Hershey or Lebanon. If your uniform wasn't perfect and your shoes weren't shined, the MP's kicked you off the bus and you had the pleasure of taking the long walk back to the barracks. In Hershey, we went to the park to enjoy the rides and see the big bands playing at the park's dance hall. When the bus went to Lebanon, I'd go to Jean Baumholder's house, change into my civvies, then we'd go to Pushnik's to drink a few beers, eat a couple of liverwurst sandwiches, and get in a dance or two.

Doing our part to play the soldiers that we really weren't, we went to the rifle range to fire our carbines. I wasn't too bad of a shot and I managed to hit the target fairly regularly. While at the range, a lieutenant ordered my brother Lou and I to stand guard at the road leading to the range. We had written instructions not to let any vehicles go down the dangerous road that led to the target pits. All went well until a silver-haired colonel, who thought he was pretty hot stuff, pulled up in a jeep.

"What's going on here, boy?" He asked.

"I'm sorry, sir. No vehicles are allowed to go down this road," I said.

"What do mean no vehicles are allowed on the road? What the hell is going on here? Do you have written orders?"

"Yes, sir," I replied.

"Well, don't just stand there. Let me see them." He demanded.

After studying the orders as if they were an examination, he roared, "What is this anyway, can't you read?"

I replied, "Yes, sir. I go to Penn State University. And I can read quite well, sir."

He ignored the orders and commanded his jeep driver to keep going down the road. I was sorry that I didn't have a bullet, because if I had one, he would have needed a new tire.

At the end of the day, the officer who ordered Lou and I to guard the road had forgotten about us. We were left guarding a road that no one was using, and there wasn't another human being within a mile of the place. We waited over an hour past the time we should have been picked up, then we decided to abandon our posts and hit the road. We hiked a mile or so before an army truck drove by and picked us up. The private drove us to our barracks where First Sergeant DeAngelo greeted us with, "What happened to you guys?"

One of the good deals at Indiantown Gap Military Reservation was the post-exchange. At the PX, tax-free items could be bought for a pittance of the off-base price. Beer, shaving cream, and candy, were really cheap. A few of the guys in the band bought prophylactics for ten cents a package. I thought it was a pretty good deal, so I went to the PX to stock up on the rubbers just in case I ever got lucky. Since they were only a dime, I bought thirty of them for three dollars. After returning to the barracks, I stuck the rubbers in my suitcase and then I forgot about them. A week after I got back home, my mother, for some reason, opened the suitcase that was under my bed and saw the prophylactics. Shocked by her discovery, she demanded to know with whom I was having an affair.

I said, "No one. But if I ever got lucky, I'd use them."

Mother lectured me, and then she pulled the silent treatment until I took the damned things out of my suitcase and threw them in the trash. But not before I stuck one in my wallet.

Who knows? I might just get lucky one of these days, I said to myself

Looking For A Teaching Job

About to graduate from Penn State, I had an interview with a school district near Philadelphia. The night before the interview, I stayed at a classmate's house in the City of Brotherly Love. The next day, I went to the meeting with the principal of the Huntington Valley Elementary School, but I was not aware that the school was in a restricted area. This translated into no blacks, Italians, or Jews were permitted to live there. Once the principal saw me, his jaw dropped a couple of inches, then he picked up the telephone and called the school board president. Twenty minutes later, the board president came over to the school in her riding breeches, leather boots, a cream colored blouse, and a whip. After confirming his suspicion that I was a Jew, the principal showed me around the area then dismissed me forever. At that point, my search for a school teaching position seemed like a lost cause, so I decided that it really wasn't worth the effort.

Carlisle, Pennsylvania

After graduating from Penn State, I moved to Harrisburg, and with the help of my Jewish landlady, we phoned around to several places in search of a job. We hit gold when I received a offer from Corvettes, a wholesale department store. I was assigned to the pharmaceutical department, and for eight hours a day, whenever customers attempted to buy nationally known brands, I pushed them to buy our products.

"Look at this label. It says Corvettes, but it is exactly the same as Preparation H," I said.

I also resupplied the inventory, ordered pills, and a host of other duties that left me exhausted at the end of each day. I earned $40.00 a week before taxes; hardly a fortune even in those days. At night, I would dream that I was working, and that made for an exhausting twenty-four hours.

During early August, while at work, I received a phone call from the Carlisle School District. The superintendent asked if I was interested in a teaching position that a classmate of mine backed out of when he accepted a job in his hometown of Hershey, Pennsylvania.

"Yes, I'll take it. Just send me the contract and I'll sign it."

I was teaching at Mt. Holly Springs Elementary School, a small town located midway between Carlisle and Gettysburg, when I made friends with Ed Wheatland and Catlin George. He became my roommate, and Catlin was my girlfriend. Ed was about five-feet nine-inches tall, a thin frame, and had brown eyes and curly hair. He was nice guy who taught music in a neighboring district. Being a Indiana State College graduate, he knew my pals, Jack Colbert and Jake Dellinger. Catlin, a warm and attractive girl, who always dressed to kill, had a Mediterranean face with a pretty nose, big brown eyes, and a shape that any man would admire. Catlin was a Greek-American who taught English at Carlisle

High School. During the summer months, I'd spend my weekends at Catlin's two story house in Carlisle where neither of her parents, who only spoke Greek, could maneuver up to the second floor because they were too fat from eating the food they served at their restaurant.

During my year in Carlisle, I renewed my friendship with my cousin, Irving "Butch" Kaminski. Butch was in Baltimore, Maryland, about an hour and a half away, so it was a quick trip to drive my Karmann Ghia to Baltimore to see him. Irving was a navy veteran, and at the time, he was selling new cars. On those weekends, besides eating in a bar the featured plates of shrimp and fried chicken, we would visit various jazz clubs and strip joints.

Irving and I walked into a jazz club, and although there were nearly a hundred people in the place, we were the only white guys in the drinking establishment. Sitting next to the bandstand was a large table occupied by four girls who seemed to be having a great time drinking and listening to the music. They looked over at us and smiled. After returning their smiles, they invited us to sit down at their table. And now six of us were having a good time. A few moments later, I happened to look over my shoulder, and that is when I spotted three guys slowly heading in our direction.

"Hey, Butch. Is your hospitalization paid for?"

"Why do you ask?" Irving wondered.

"There are three guys walking over here. And they are all wearing key chains, hats, and zoot suits," I said.

"Oh, Christ!" He moaned.

They stood directly behind us for about thirty seconds, then one of the guys tapped me on the shoulder. My guess was that we were going to have to fight our way out of the joint.

"Hey buddy," whispered the guy who tapped me on the shoulder.

"Yes," I answered nervously.

"The girl sitting next to you has the crabs," he whispered.

"Man! Thanks for telling me." I was happy that those guys didn't want to beat the hell out of us. And that is when I suggested, "Why don't you guys sit down and have a couple of drinks with us?"

"Sure. That would be real cool," he answered.

For the rest of the evening, the nine of us enjoyed listening to the music, talking, and drinking beer together.

Ed Wheatland and I drove to Baltimore see the famous stripper, Blue Star. It must have been my lucky night because I was chosen by Miss Star to go up onto the stage and unzip the back of her dress. Not accustomed to performing such deeds, I was a bit nervous when I started to undo her dress, and that is when the darn thing got stuck. I gave it my best shot, but I couldn't get the blasted thing down. Blue, after telling me to hurry up and unzip her dress, finally grew disgusted and ordered me to get the hell off her stage. The customers were really pissed. They booed and threw beer bottles at me as I shamefully fled from the stage.

Ed who was from Meadville, Pennsylvania, the very place where the zippers were made, told Miss Star, "You can get a refund if you write to them," he announced.

"Shut up!" I said. "Let's get the hell out of here while we still can."

New York City

Traveling to New York City a couple of weekends every month from Carlisle, I decided to move to New York's East Seventy-First Street to share an apartment with Ray Miller and Steve Sokel. I resigned from the Carlisle School District, and after going to a teacher placement agency where I paid an arm and a leg to have them set-up an interview, I received an offer from the Babylon School District and I accepted the position. Before leaving Carlisle, according to a friend of mine, the school superintendent said to everyone working in the office, "So, Mr. Getz is going to teach on Long Island with the rest of the Jews!"

Ray and I got along quite well, but Steve, who was Jewish, and also from Altoona, was an unmitigated pain in the ass. After a couple of months in Manhattan's east side, we moved to the Queens. One dark and stormy night, I punched Steve out after he repeatedly bated me about a number of things. Several times, I had warned him to stop, but he kept on with his nasty comments. Finally, I punched him then wrestled him to the floor. After a couple of minutes, the fight ended in my favor. The final result was that both Ray and I were elated when Sokel moved upstairs to another apartment.

It was just before the 1961 Christmas vacation when I had an epiphany. My sixth grade students, a terrific group of kids were bored as hell with their state mandated reading books, but we plodded along like a group of mechanical automatons. In an attempt to motivate my students, I came up with an idea that just might stimulate them to read some of America's best literature. What if I bought books at a bookstore in the city and we would study from them? The kids immediately liked the idea, and during the Christmas break, I purchased the books at a subway bookstore. My first acquisition was "African Treasury," by Langston Hughes. They loved the novel, and memorized some of his poems. Another of Hughes

61

books that we read was "The Dream Keeper." Some of the other books that we studied were J.D. Salinger's "Catcher In The Rye," "A Perfect Day For A Banana Fish," Seymour, and, "Raise The Roof Beam High." The class really loved Hughes and Salinger, but the irritated principal told me that we had to use the state reading text. In any event, I had stimulated the kids to read quality books, probably for the rest of lives.

Taking a train from Lebanon, Pennsylvania to New York City, Jean Baumholder was about to experience life as I knew it in the big city. Meeting her at the train station and greeting her with a kiss, we headed up Broadway when, for some reason, she stopped at a phone booth to make a call to Lebanon. Something told me that it wasn't her mother that she was phoning. After she finished her call, we walked for another ten minutes before she, once again, made another call. Another ten minutes went by before Jean had her third telephone conversation. After she finished talking on the phone, she said, "Harv, I've got to go back to Lebanon."

I tried my best to talk her out of returning to Lebanon, but I couldn't convince her to do otherwise. With plans to go to the Five Spot, Charlie's Bar, the White Horse Cafe, and my favorite delicatessen, as well as some other places, I was disappointed with her decision. Sadly, I walked Jean back to the train station to say goodbye to her and a once promising vacation. That evening, I went to Charlie's Bar and sat next to Gerry Mulligan. Although we didn't talk or even acknowledge each other, I can still say that we had a few beers together.

Not everything was fun and games in New York. Late one afternoon, when I still owned my Karmann Ghia, I was coming home from work and rounded a corner near my apartment in the Queens. The guy driving behind me beeped his horn, slammed on his brakes, and then jumped out of his car and ran up to my car window. I had stopped to see what was wrong, and the problem was that I wasn't going fast enough for him. That's when he decided to punch me out for going around a corner at a moderate speed. Through the driver's side of the window, I looked up at the guy and he looked as crazy as mad hatter. His eyes were all red, his skin was pale, and his hair looked like it had just been through a windstorm. Although he skinny as a snake, I figured that he was high on something, so I didn't want to fight him. The guy was pounding on my window and shouting obscenities. That is when I rolled down the window just enough so that his arm fit partially through the opening. At that point, he tried to throw a punch, but I quickly rolled the window back up to the closed position. With his arm now trapped halfway in the window, I started the car then slowly drove down the street with the screaming fellow attached to my automobile. I traveled a little over a city block with the guy shouting obscenities at me and shaking his left fist. When it was safe to do, I released him, then sped down the road to the safety of my apartment.

Listening to Miles Davis, Count Basic, Joe Williams, Stan Getz, John Coltrane, and James Moody at the local jazz clubs was one of my favorite pastimes. James Moody was a fellow who could really play the alto, tenor and soprano saxophones the way they should be played. The first time I went to the Five Spot to hear him, I was completely mesmerized by his sound and technique, and the guy could really swing. I sat at the wooden bar with my eyes closed digging everything he was doing. When the quartet took their break, he walked over to talk to me.

"So you like the music?" He asked.

"Of course I do. It's really great. And I dug that last tune, "Autumn Leaves," I replied.

During the intermission, we talked about jazz, but mostly I talked about his style of playing.

"Are you gonna' be here until the next break?" He asked.

"I sure am."

"How about for the rest of the night?" He wondered.

"I'm sticking around until you are finished," I answered.

"That's good. After I finish my gig, what do you say we walk to the subway together and talk some more," James said.

"Sure. That would be great," I answered.

For the next few months, James Moody and I walked to the subway stop, about four blocks from the Five Spot, then we rode together until we got to Times Square. Once there, James changed to the "A" train up to Harlem, and I took the Flushing Meadows subway train back to the Queens.

Deciding that I had much to learn, I enrolled in a black history course at the New School of Social Research. As far as I could tell, it was one of the first courses of its kind in the United States. The only drawback was that I didn't have the money to pay for the tuition. After meeting with Abbey Lincoln, curriculum coordinator, singer, movie star, and wife of jazz drummer, Max Roach, I was given free tuition to take the course.

All I had to do was take the attendance each week and submit it to the main office. What a deal!

Our teacher was Afro-American man named Robert Priestly, who happened to be a fairly well known classical pianist and local bon vivant. For some strange reason, he decided that I was the white guy who had the right stuff to write about the black experience. For a couple of months, I went to a few gatherings and hung out at his Harlem apartment. One of the parties was up in Harlem, and *Le plat principal* was barbecued pigeon. Since there were over a hundred guests, and they were being served in groups of twenty people, I had enough time to get out of there and go for a bite to eat at a bar down the street. When it was getting close to my turn to find a seat at the table, I made my discreet exit from the pigeon-filled brownstone house. A few minutes later, I entered the bar, and sitting there was the great jazz pianist, Randy Easton, and one of Robert Priestly's writing pals. They were both laughing their asses off at me because they didn't want to eat the damn pigeons either!

The time had come for me to write the paper, but I was really having a hard time getting my thoughts together. At the time, I simply didn't have any idea what Dr. Priestly wanted from me, but I finally scribbled some things down and submitted it to him. A week later, I went up to Harlem to see him, and when I knocked on the door, and his boyfriend answered, but he refused to let me to see him. A long story made short, Robert Priestly wanted nothing to do with the paper or me.

My feeble attempt to write on the black experience was an unmitigated failure, and I felt awful about disappointing him, but a week later, I got over it and continued on with my life in big city.

There were many women who were very special to me, but Catlin and Christine George were special to me. Working for Columbia Records as a secretary, Christine, who occasionally danced on Broadway and had a lively personality, was the older of the two sisters. Although she smoked like a campfire, she was very attractive and had the kind of looks that could capture and hold onto a man's heart. Her long, black hair flowed down to her shoulders, and her slightly bronzed skin covered an almost perfect body. On the other hand, Catlin, who didn't smoke, was a very kind and sweet girl who taught school, and as I mentioned earlier, was also a good-looking woman. Since my days in Carlisle, I had been dating Catlin, but I discovered that I also was very interested in going out with her sister. Christine and I would meet on Friday afternoons in a bar just below the Columbia Record Studios where we enjoyed a few drinks before taking long walks on the streets of Manhattan. One rainy night, a drunken fellow came to up us to tell me how lucky I was to have her as my girlfriend. It could have been love, but I couldn't choose one without hurting the other. Being left with the choice of hurting Catlin's feelings in order to pursue Christine, I did the only thing I could do, I gave up both sisters.

Barbara Goldberg was a girl I had dated at Penn State, but during her sophomore year, Barbara transferred to Boston University because she believed that they offered a better program in journalism. Three years had gone by since I last saw her, but it was a chance meeting at a New York coffee shop where I ran into her again. She was a slim redhead with a pretty face that came with brown eyes, smooth skin, and a petite body. Barbara was working for TV Guide as a writer assigned to interview celebrities. One of those celebrities those she had recently interviewed was none other than the king of rock and roll, Elvis Presley. Although Barbara had a boyfriend, we started dating again, that is, until one evening at my apartment when she asked me a loaded question.

"Harv, have you ever thought about making love to me?"

I knew it was a question full of traps, and not an invitation for a wrestling match in the hay.

"No, I haven't given it much thought," I lied.

She pondered over what I said, then challenged me to tell the truth. "Do you mean even if I asked you to do it, would you?"

Apparently, her boyfriend had warned her that all men were horny bastards who would do anything to get into a girl's pants. Now I was trapped between a rock and a hard place.

I answered, "Well, if you asked me to, then I guess that I would do it. But only if you asked me to," I assured her.

Now she was pissed, "You mean to tell me that you would go to bed with me if I asked you to? I think that is just plain awful. Harv, I think you had better take me home."

There was no way I could win the argument; her virginity was safely intact for at least another night.

A couple of weeks later, I went to a party in Manhattan where Barbara Goldberg was talking with a group of hopeful female would-be writers. After seeing her with the girls sitting around in a circle hanging onto her every word, in the privacy of a dark and distant corner, I asked her to knock it off and stop acting like she had all the answers for those misbegotten girls.

"I'm just trying to help them by sharing a few pointers," she said.

It was a little later that evening, Barbara told me that she was getting married. But she quickly added that we could still be friends.

"No thanks. You know it is all or nothing with me."

Barbara Goldberg was a Jewish girl that I might have fallen in love with, but she had made her choice and I wished her nothing the best.

A good-looking Protestant-Irish girl with an incredible sense of humor was my next girlfriend. Helen McGee and I spent a couple of fun-filled months playing tricks on each other, and we had a hell of a good time doing it. One evening after work, I took the Long Island railroad train into the city to meet her for an early evening cocktail at the plush Hotel New Yorker. After we sat down at a table next to a large bay window, we ordered our whiskey sours. But a few minutes later, she suddenly felt ill.

"Harv, I really feel nauseous. I think I better go to the ladies room," said the fairly tall brunette with eyes that shined like a pair of rubies.

"I hope everything is all right," I said.

"Don't worry. I'll be OK in a few minutes," she replied.

As Helen got up to go to the rest room, her hand covered her pretty mouth. Then, without so much as a warning, she barfed all over the maroon carpet that covered the floor of the bar. Suddenly, all the drinkers stopped talking and looked down at the gooey mess. To say that the pathetic sight upset everyone in the place was an understatement. But without a trace of embarrassment, she reached down and pulled the vomit off the carpeted floor. I'll be damned if it wasn't a trick rubber device complete with chunks of ersatz meat and flies attached to it. Everybody in the place got a big laugh out of it before turning back to their drinks and conversations.

I asked Helen to get dressed to kill because we were going to a very special place for dinner. Excited by the prospect of eating at a plush steak house, she borrowed a mink stole from her aunt. After meeting her at her house, we were off to a distant subway stop to enjoy a couple of kosher hot dogs and cokes.

Things continued to go swimmingly until one evening at our usual Friday night pub, just a couple of blocks from her Brooklyn Heights home, we were sitting with another couple enjoying an evening of beer drinking and conversation. That is, until she saw her former boyfriend standing at the bar. From what her married friends whispered to me, he was on home leave from the army. Seeing him standing alone at the bar, she excused herself and sauntered over to say a few words to him. Helen was still talking to the fellow and hour later, and that is when I realized that our days of romance and playing tricks on each other had come to an end. After she returned to the table, Helen asked me to take a walk outside with her. Just around the corner from the tavern, we stopped in front of an elegant house surrounded by shrubs and trees. She hesitated for a minute before saying, "Harv, I am sorry, but I'm going to marry John." There was a hint of sympathy, but from the sound of her voice, she had made up her mind to marry him. I also got the impression that she wanted to get her goodbye over with and get back to finish up with their marriage plans.

"When are you planning on getting married?" I asked.

"We are getting married this Saturday," she replied.

"That soon? Well, I guess it would be a useless to try and talk you out of it. It sounds like you've made up your mind and there is nothing I can do about it. So I guess this is goodbye, Helen McGee." I turned and left her standing on the darkened steps. My heart was heavy, but I knew a well-executed "goodbye Harv," when I saw one. I walked a couple of blocks to the subway then took the train to the Five Spot where I got stinking drunk.

Helen's final joke was on me.

Katie McNabb was an attractive girl with a wholesome look accentuated by her blond hair, blue eyes, and nice body. When I first met Katie, a third grade teacher at my school, she seemed to be a bit unhappy with the way things were going in her life. It was after school on a Friday afternoon, and while walking by her room, I noticed that she was sitting at her desk with her pretty head between her soft hands.

"Hello there. I must say that you seem to be upset about something." It was the first time that I had spoken to her since coming to Babylon Elementary School.

"I'm bored," she moaned. "You know, I really feel stuck out here in Babylon. There really isn't anything to do here."

I replied, "So why don't you come to the city sometime," I suggested. "I'd be more than happy to show you around. Why I'd even take you to a jazz club."

Katie smiled for the first time, "I just might do that one of these days."

"Well, here is my phone number. Please call me any time you want to come to the city." I said.

The following day, after finishing my morning coffee, I received an unexpected phone call.

"Hello, Harv. This is Katie McNabb. I'm coming to the city today. That is, if you have time to show me around," she said.

"Wow! That was sure a quick decision. Yes, of course," I said.

A few hours later, she arrived at my apartment. We had a cup of coffee and chatted a bit before taking the subway into Manhattan to have a bite to eat. We went to a small Italian restaurant for dinner, and afterwards, we found our way to the White Horse Cafe to discuss the meaning of life with a table full of total strangers. Our final stop for the evening was the Five Spot where we enjoyed the sounds of trumpeter, Donald Byrd. By the time we got back to my apartment, it was around 2:00 AM. Because it was getting to be morning, and her place was at least an hour away, I was worried about her driving back to Babylon.

"Why don't you stay at my place for the night. I've got clean pajamas, a fresh toothbrush, and I'll sleep out on the couch. Besides, there is plenty of room because my roommates have gone away for the weekend."

After some persuading, Katie finally agreed to stay over at my place. The next morning, I made breakfast, then we went into Manhattan to my favorite delicatessen for a pastrami sandwich. After lunch, we returned to my apartment for a final cup of coffee before she drove back to boring Babylon.

I don't remember how I found out about the Overseas Schools, but it was sometime in the early spring when I went for a job interview. Squeezed between the other monstrous concrete structures on Wall Street, I entered the Federal Building thinking that it was going to be a one-on-one interview. Instead, approximately two hundred people were sitting in metal chairs preparing to listen to a fellow wearing thick glasses, a cheap brown suit, and a conservative blue bow tie. *A government worker if I ever saw one,* I thought to myself.

"Overseas," the civil servant began, "you may be working in places where the natives don't want you there." He paused to see if anyone was getting up to leave, but no one did. "And you'll be teaching in places with diseases and sicknesses that you never heard of before." Still, no one left the room.

Going around in my head was the tune "I May Be Wrong", as he droned on about living overseas. Then, I thought to myself, *there are approximately two hundred people sitting in folding chairs listening to this guy. Not much chance getting a job with the Overseas Schools, but what the hell!*

"How many of you people are married?" The government man asked. At least a hundred hands went up. "Well, I have to be honest with you. We aren't taking married teachers at this time. However, you can interview if you want to, but you'll not going to work for the Overseas Schools," he advised.

As if a starting pistol had gone off in the room, over one hundred strangely silent New Yorkers got up from their metal chairs and headed out the door.

Well, my chances have just doubled, I said to myself.

A few weeks later, I received an offer from the U.S. Air Force for a teaching position in Libya, but I turned it down and waited for another offer. Frankly, Libya wasn't a good place for a Jewish kid. At that time, each branch of the service had its own schools, so I could conceivably receive three offers. A couple of weeks later, I got a Saturday morning telegram from the Army offering me a position on the island of Okinawa.

"Should I take the job?" I asked Katie, who was staying at my place for the weekend.

"I don't know. It's up to you," she answered.

"I'll tell you what," I said, "I'm going to flip a coin, and if it's heads, then I'll accept the position."

I secretly maneuvered the coin so that it would flip to heads.

"Well, that's it. I'm going to Okinawa," I declared.

Two months later, Katie resigned her teaching position in Babylon to begin a new life in San Francisco. She phoned me from her home in Poughkeepsie and offered to drive me across the country to the Golden Gate City. Strange things could happen along the way, but I would resist the urge to do anything rash if I could help it. Besides, Katie said that she wanted to begin a new life.

I asked my contact person if it would be all right if I drove out to San Francisco with a friend instead of taking an airplane. Her answer was firm and unequivocal. "I'm afraid not. You must be ready to leave on a twenty-four hour notice." She paused for effect. "And you must leave from New York City. By the way, if you get married, the deal is off," she warned.

How did she know that I wanted to drive out to California with a woman?

Aboard The USNS Sultan

Following my three day stay at San Francisco's Fort Mason Officers Quarters, and going to Alioto's for lunch everyday to leer at Maria wearing her low-cut dirndl and bellowing out German songs with Fritz, the accordion player, I hailed a cab to the Oakland Army Terminal. After arriving at the port, I walked up the gangplank of the USS *Sultan* with my suitcase, the one with the Penn State sticker on it, and was escorted to my cabin by a member of the crew. The room was furnished with three double decker beds, a shelf for underwear, and a couple of pieces of steel furniture for clothes. There were no pictures, mirrors or curtains. After getting a good look at what was going to be my home for the next twenty days, I went back up the ladder to the main deck to view the departure proceedings. By that time, I noted that several people had come aboard the ship and were being escorted to their cabins by members of the *Sultan's* staff. On the pier, an Army band was tuning up while a gathering of people were waiting to watch the vessel depart for our voyage to Okinawa.

Thirty minutes later, the band played, "My Bonnie Lies Over The Ocean", while those spectators on the quay held onto one end of the stringers and the ship's passengers grasped the other end of the ribbons. My shipmates continued to hold them until the crepe paper decorations sunk into the sea. Following the impressive farewell ceremony, I went back to my cabin to meet my roommates. Now, there were three of us occupying the spartan cabin. After introducing ourselves, we quickly became friends, and it only took a few minutes for humor to find its way into our conversation. I learned the two teachers came from different parts of the country, Tony, a fellow who was quick to tell a joke, was from the northern part of the United States. Jim, on the hand, had a more subtle sense of humor, and he was from the southern part of the country. Tony, who was about five feet eight, had wavy hair, and was a bit muscular. Jim, on the other hand, was a tall redhead, thin, and must have been a neatness freak because his underwear and socks were already neatly folded and stored on his shelf.

That evening, we were assigned seats at a dining table, and as luck would have it, my cabin mates and I were sitting with some good-looking women, Ruth Grant, Connie Waite, and Susan Francis. Ruth was a pleasant young woman with the propensity to be kind in the way that could drive men crazy. A prim and proper attractive girl from Hendricks, Minnesota, Connie Waite sat just to the right of me. In spite of my New York dating experience, I wasn't sure how to approach Connie. She was a good Christian girl endowed with the values that came with being religious, and that made me somewhat unsure of myself. Nevertheless, I found her very attractive. She had curly blond hair, and was easy to imagine her in a bathing suit instead of the very proper dress that she was wearing. Another attractive girl, Susan Francis, who hailed from southern California, was also sitting at our table, and she was far less inhibited by her religion. She was also a blond, and she had everything that the Beach Boys were singing about. For the next twenty days, we ate four times a day, exercised together at the Harv Getz Health Club, and sunbathed in the Pacific sun. After being out to sea for a few days, I got up a band and we performed at the eight o'clock evening buffets. The drummer, after interviewing about forty Marines, was the only one who could play a paradiddle, so he got the job. It was too bad that no matter what song we were playing, he beat his drum to the exact thumping of the ships engines. The ship's engineer played a pretty mean jazz fiddle, the heavy-set pianist was on his way to Japan to be a music teacher, and yours truly was on the saxophone. We weren't that good, but we gave it our best shot, and our shipmates enjoyed the music.

Yokohama

After eighteen days on the high seas, we pulled into the city of Yokohama where the passengers, after eighteen days at sea, were given twenty-four hours of liberty in the Japanese city. This was just enough time for my roommates and I to walk around the town and take in some of the awesome sites. While walking down a busy sidewalk, I noted that it felt good to be one of the tallest guys in town, even though I was only five feet nine inches tall. On our tour of the city, we witnessed bare-breasted old women sitting in front of electric fans trying to cool themselves, food hawkers selling their goods on the street, and small stores peddling just about everything under the sun. A little later, we saw a group of half-naked fellows shouting, *Wa-Shoi*! *Wa-Shoi!* while parading around the city streets carrying an *Omikoshi* shrine.

Mixed with the hot and humid air that permeated the town, was the sweet smell of incense when I suddenly whined, "I could really use a cold beer about now."

"Speaking of cold beers, I think there is a place up there where we can get one," Jim said.

We looked up at the three-story building, and I was amazed to see a bar on the second floor.

"By golly. I think you're right," Tony exclaimed.

After walking up the long flight of wooden steps that left us nearly out of breath, we strolled into the place. The drinking establishment was quite large, and like many joints in the states, it was air-conditioned and had a long bar. On the wall behind the bar were the usual neon signs advertising the various available brews. But they had different names from the ones in America. Instead of Millers, Schlitz, and Budweiser, they sold Kirin, Asahi, and Sapporo beers. The beverages were totally unfamiliar to us, but we were more than willing to give them a try. Hoping they would be cold, we sat down at the bar and ordered three Sapporo beers. No sooner were the nearly frozen beers placed in front of us, when, as if we had rubbed genie bottles instead of a beer bottles, three good looking girls suddenly appeared.

"Where did you girls come from? It's like you were beamed down to us!" Tony exclaimed.

"We fairy princess," one of the girls claimed.

The women stood next to us at the bar, and we ordered three more beers for them. After introducing ourselves, we moved to a table and spoke of absurdities until somewhere in the middle of the laughing and clowning around, I remembered a line from a Korean War novel that I recently read. The main character in the story, while sitting in a bar, asked a Japanese girl, "You be my number one skivvy honcho?" Out of my mouth came those exact words, and without hesitation, the three girls got up from the table, grabbed our hands, and led us out of the bar. That was the beginning of a friendship that lasted for the remainder of the day. We went to a bathhouse, stripped down to our birthday suits, and enjoyed splashing around in the hot bath together. Later, we followed up with a delicious meal at a small restaurant. Afterwards, well I won't say what happened afterwards, but it was certainly enjoyable.

Before leaving our slightly worn-out hotel, we threw our stolen kimonos out a back window, then we went out into the moonlit night to retrieve them, but we quickly discovered that there were walls surrounding every house in the neighborhood. Those seven-foot walls, with broken glass cemented on the top, prevented petty thieves like us from recovering our stolen *bingatas*. As we were pondering the barrier, a group of Japanese guys. wearing judo outfits, spotted us from a half a block away. They shouted something, then began chasing us down the unpaved dark alleyway. We managed to escape the angry Japanese fellows by jumping into a cab and telling the driver to take us back to the safety of our ship.

Early the next morning, Connie Waite wanted to see some of Yokohama before we departed for Okinawa. The two of us left the ship and hailed a cab to the center of the city. As far as the driver was concerned, we were just a couple of tourists out for Saturday morning joyride. Little did we know that the cabbie was a proud owner of "a Kamikaze Cab." The hell on wheels driver nearly frightened us to death throughout our agonizing ordeal. Connie was so frightened that she grabbed my hand and held on to it while the death-defying cabbie went the wrong way on one-way streets, sped over numerous curbs, and nearly crashed into a couple of honey carts (horse drawn carts carrying human feces). Eventually, much to our relief, the grinning driver got us back to the USS *Sultan* in time for our noon departure.

Okinawa At Last!

Leaning on the railing of the main deck as the ship slowly sailed into the port of Naha, I said to the soldier standing next to me, "Well, Lieutenant Kelly, Okinawa at last!"

The bespectacled former Marine's myopia was a problem when he applied for a Marine commission, but the Army was more than happy to have him as an officer, poor eyesight and all.

"Indeed, my friend. We are finally here," he said.

I pointed to a distant hill that was as barren as an elderly woman's womb. Because it had been pounded with artillery shells during the war, it was absent of anything that might have given it some character.

"Although it has been seventeen years since the war, the hills still show a lot of damage," Lieutenant Kelly observed.

"They sure do," I agreed.

Spotting a couple of local guys fishing on a large rock, I shouted, "Now if that isn't a sight for sorry eyes. Look at those two fisherman over there!" Both were wearing big straw hats, cut off fatigue pants, old US army shirts, and wide grins on their wrinkled faces.

What the hell have I gotten myself into, anyway? Okinawa seemed as foreign to me as Mars or some other distant planet. This certainly wasn't New York, I thought to myself.

After disembarking from the USNS *Sultan,* we were greeted by our principal, Mr. Howard Thomas. He was a somewhat elderly gentleman, and what was left of his gray hair, was blowing in the slight breeze. Dressed in a Hawaiian shirt, a pair of khaki shorts, leather sandals, and a smile as wide as a football field, the middle-aged principal looked as if he had lived on Okinawa for a long time.

"Miss Turner, Miss Francis, and Mr. Getz, I'm your principal. Let me be the first to welcome you all to Okinawa," he said.

"Thank you. It's a pleasure to be here," we chorused.

We walked to his car and climbed into the backseat of the principal's Nash. Slightly dented, it reminded me of my Uncle Aaron's car back in Altoona, except my uncle's car was in a lot better shape and much cleaner. The principal started the car, then pulled out onto the main road, Highway One. He switched on a tiny fan that was attached to the steering column that cooled no one except himself. The weather was extremely hot and humid, and Mr. Thomas warned us that the weather would remain that way until the middle of October.

Reaching down to the floor near the gas pedal, he grabbed a thermos mug and unscrewed the top. "Anybody want a martini," he offered.

I thought to myself, *so you are a boozer, eh?*

"No, thank you," we chanted.

On both sides of the road were military surplus shops stocked with helmets, uniforms, tires, and a collection of stuff that made you wonder who bought those things anyway. As we sped up the highway, we caught a view of the East China Sea. A little later, we drove past the turnoff where Mr. Thomas mumbled something about a helicopter base. We kept going straight ahead for another one-half mile, and at the intersection, he made a right turn and went up a hill through the dusty town of Futeema. Through the dirty windshield, I saw an old movie theatre where the featured presentation was "Brakefast at Tiffany's." Although it was misspelled on the marquee, I made a mental note of the movie and planned to see it when I had a chance. Just past the village was Camp Sukiran. We took another right turn and entered the gate that was guarded by an Okinawan. Weaponless, except for the karate stick attached to his belt, the guard checked the principal's identification card then waved us through the gate. A half minute later, just before we drove past the coffee shop, Mr. Thomas, who was now slurring from his martinis, pointed out our school to us.

"Down the hill is Sukiran Elementary School. It looks very nice, doesn't it?" Commented the now intoxicated principal.

"Yes, it does." Susan replied.

"Before we do anything else," the principal said, "we are going to a party at the BOQ to welcome you all."

"What's a BOQ?" Ruth asked.

Since Susan's father had been a naval officer and was involved in the planning of *operation iceberg*, the battle for Okinawa, she already knew the answer.

"Bachelors Officers Quarters," she answered. "That's where we will be living."

Although there were a couple of screw ups at the party, for example, the principal forgot to get me a place stay, but other than that, things were going well until Susan announced that we were going to the officers club to meet a friend for dinner. Now completely drunk, Mr. Thomas grabbed Susan's arm and warned her that no one left his party until he said they could leave. I straightened the principal out on the matter, then both of us left the soiree and hailed a cab to the club.

The moment we stepped into the Top of the Rock we discovered that it was very plush place furnished in Chinese decor, including a couple of expensive lacquer screens, a scattering of oriental lamps, several large porcelain jars, and windows covered by drapes that were worthy of a queen. The floors were covered with elaborate Chinese carpets that were beautiful pieces of art. In fact, the club was so elegant that it was included for its opulence in the novel, "The Ugly American."

Susan Francis and I met the handsome ensign from the USNS *Sultan* in the lobby of the club, then we went searching for an unoccupied table. After finding one, we sat down to enjoy an evening of scrumptious food and wonderful entertainment. When the waitress came to our table, we ordered three steak dinners and a bottle of red wine. Playing that night was a thirteen-piece Filipino dance band and a couple of singers who more that capable of carrying a tune. The ensign danced with Susan a few times, we ate our dinner, sipped the wine, and talked until we ran out of things to say. The unwelcome silence was the cue for the ensign to catch a taxi back to the *Sultan,* then on to whatever destiny had in store for him. As for Susan and I, we returned to the principal's party where, later in the evening, the social director told me not to worry about where I was going to sleep tonight, because she found a place for me to stay.

Early the next morning, I met Susan Francis and Kay White, a teacher from Sukiran Elementary School, for breakfast at the coffee shop. After having pancakes and coffee, we left Kay and her pancakes for our maiden voyage to Naha. Staring out the window of the crowded bus, we revisited the junk and pawnshops we saw yesterday, and noted several new places of interest, including the Pizza House, and the James S. Lee Tailors. As we approached the outskirts of the city, the bus swerved and we nearly collided with an unlikely pair of animals; a water buffalo and a swaybacked horse. The odd couple was pulling a wooden flatbed wagon attached to a pair of jeep wheels. The man's bare feet hung over the back of cart as if he were soaking them in a tub of hot water. A conical shaped straw hat and parts of an army surplus uniform protected him from the blazing hot sun. His bronze face broke out into a wonderful Okinawan smile as he joyfully returned our wave.

After reaching the top of Shuri Hill, we got off the bus and walked around the ruins of the fourteenth century castle. Reduced to rubble and mounds of stones, the fortress was destroyed in the "Typhoon of Steel" during the war. For an hour, we roamed around the area examining rocks and looking at what was left of the once great structure. Then we started down the hill where we passed a couple of small houses with rocks piled on top of their roofs. Those small boulders kept the sheets of metal from blowing away during typhoons. We also looked at a tiny wooden store with a pathetically small inventory made up of a can of Spam, a white radish, a couple of eggs, and some greens. Finally arriving at the bottom of the hill, we found ourselves on *Kokusai* Street, the main street of Naha.

The busy tree-lined street was lined with jewelry, lacquerware, and clothing shops, as well as a movie theatre, three department stores, several restaurants, and coffee shops where people congregated to listen to music and chat. We continued walking down the street until we discovered an outdoor market located next to a polluted river. Later, I named it the *Kusai Kawa* (smelly river). The canvas-topped market covered an area of approximately three-square blocks. Operated by seemingly impoverished women, they enthusiastically sold vegetables, meats, fish, pots, pans, and dozens of other items, including black market products. The women, young and old, greeted us with wonderful smiles and the expression, *"atsui desu ne?"* It's hot, isn't it?

While experiencing the open market and the pleasant looks on the women's faces, Susan and I fell in love with Okinawa and her resilient people. Later in the day, we went to a restaurant and ordered a couple of steaks and a plate of fried rice. It was at the restaurant where we learned to use chopsticks by watching a couple of Okinawan men manipulate them. We copied their technique, but the steaks were so tough that we couldn't eat them. Not wanting to insult the owner, we hid the meat in Susan's pocketbook, and after we finished our meal, we gave the steaks to a dog with good teeth.

The next day, the principal rectified his mistake, and I was assigned quarters in the men's BOQ. The rooms were comprised of two bedrooms and a very narrow hallway kitchen where the airplane sized bathroom was located. My roommate lived in one of the bedrooms, and I had the other one. According to our housekeeper, the fellow who shared my quarters was out in the field and wouldn't return for a couple of weeks.

At Sukiran Elementary School, Mr. Thomas was a pretty nice fellow when he was sober. Five days a week, I walked down the hill to the school to teach my students reading, writing, social studies, geography, and arithmetic. For physical education, we went out onto the playground and quickly worked up a sweat playing in the tropical heat. Fifteen minutes later, the kids cooled off with the room's lone electric fan.

It was Saturday afternoon and I had nothing else to do, so I went to the movie theater in Futeema to see "Breakfast At Tiffany's." While watching the now classic film, I had flashbacks of my experiences in New York, and before I knew it, I was George Peppard, and Holly Golightly was Helen McGee, who looked and acted a bit like Audrey Hepburn. This marked the only time that I was homesick for The Five Spot, the New York delicatessen, the dating scene, the White Horse Cafe, and Charlie's Bar. After the movie was over, I walked out onto the dusty hot street where I sadly realized that my New York days were now history. I slowly walked back up the hill to my BOQ where I downed a beer and fell into a coma-like sleep.

One evening, in late August of 1962, while lying on my bed reading a book, a soldier, like a howling typhoon, blew into my room.

"Hello there. I'm Charley Higa. I'm your roomy." His face was lit up like a light bulb, and his grin was warm and inviting. It was an Okinawan smile.

Standing in front of me was a handsome second lieutenant in starched fatigues with airborne wings above his breast pocket. Airborne and Ranger patches were on his right sleeve. I also noted that he was an Okinawan-American and that he must have been one hell of a tough guy, even though he stood only five feet six inches tall and weighed about 135 pounds. I knew for certain that he was a fellow that I never wanted to piss off.

"Well, hello to you too," I said, "I've been waiting about two weeks to meet you. And now you are finally here," I said as I got up from my bed.

"I'm really sorry," he apologized, "but we've been out in the field for a couple of weeks."

"Well anyway, it's finally good to meet you. I hope you're going to stick around for a while," I replied.

"We are not going out to the field for another three weeks, so I guess I am going to be around for at least that long," he said.

We shot the breeze for a few minutes before Charlie offered, "Hey, I've got an idea. Let's go to the coffee shop for something to eat. We can down a couple of beers while we to know each other a little better."

I thought it was a damn good suggestion and five minutes later, we walked into the restaurant. The first view of the place was a scattering of tables and chairs that made up the bar area. It was common ground for marines and soldiers who managed to indulge in the joys of alcohol. However the two services had an intense rivalry, and they weren't taking any prisoners.

A marine shouted across the room to a soldier who was nursing a bottle of Schlitz, "Hey dogface. As you were on that!" He exclaimed. "Make that dog breath! Are you gonna' suck on that beer like a baby in his mama's loving arms, or are you going to buy a round for the warriors?

The soldier's green beret rested next to his half empty bottle of beer. "You bet your sweet ass I will. And furthermore, I can handle as many beers as you dumb-ass jarheads can drink," answered the special forces officer.

"Don't worry about those guys. They are just having a good time," Higa-san said.

"Well, it doesn't look that way to me, but I'll take your word for it," I remarked.

A nice looking Okinawan waitress, with a shape that wouldn't quit, came to our table to take our order.

"Make that two beers and two cheeseburgers. I'm buying," said my new roommate.

The mini-sized girl with a lovely smile took our order, but she lingered a bit before leaving. Somehow, I knew I wasn't the one that held her interest.

"So tell me. That gorgeous waitress seems to really like you. What's that all about?" I asked.

"Its nothing really. I'm not interested," he replied.

"Well, I think she is very interested. Every time she glances this way, she looks at you as if she found her true love or something."

During our conversation, Charlie told me some interesting things about himself. He was a second generation Okinawan whose parents left Okinawa before the war to settle in Hawaii. Although it had been a long time since Charlie's parents left Okinawa, he still had several relatives living on the island. After graduating from high school, he entered West Point with the dream of becoming the first Okinawan to graduate from the Academy. Unfortunately, during his junior year, he was called from the movie theatre ("Never So Few," starring Frank Sinatra and Gina Lollobrigida) to receive his dismissal notice for failing his chemistry class. Shamed by his inability to pass the class, Higa-san left West Point and hopped trains around the country for six months before reporting to a recruiter to enlist in the Army.

"From Hawaii, eh?" Asked the recruiting sergeant.

"Yes, sir. I'm from Honolulu," Charlie replied.

"Say. How is that bridge, anyway?" He wondered.

"What bridge is that?" Higa-san asked.

"You know, the one that goes from Hawaii to San Francisco. I imagine they have gas stations, and restaurants and stuff like that on it."

He thought about it for a moment before answering, "Yes. They sure do," Charlie lied.

Four months had passed since I first arrived on the island with a shipload of friends. Among them was the good-looking girl from Hendricks, Minnesota. Charlie was dating Connie, and he was really in love with her, but he was handicapped by his grandmother's words. For whatever reason, she believed that different races should never mix.

"If the good lord wanted people who are different from each other to marry, he would have made everyone the same." His grandmother's words haunted him throughout their budding courtship.

Walking down the nearly deserted street between Goya and Koza on a cool Sunday afternoon, I related something to Charlie that just might have loosened the strings that tied him to his grandmother's beliefs. Borrowing an idea from Bertrand Russell's book, "Why I Am Not A Christian," I said, "I don't pretend to know what God is thinking, but, like everyone else, I can only speculate on his grand design. Horses can't make it with cows, and cats can't reproduce with dogs. But do you know what? All humans can mate with each other regardless of race."

A few months later, Connie and Charlie Higa were married in Hendricks, Minnesota.

While on a military bus to Nago, Mr. Thomas sipped one martini too many from his thermos bottle, then he proceeded to curse out a group of American women. One of the women happened to be married to a colonel, and two weeks later, Howard Thomas was booted off the island by the commanding general for conduct unbecoming a principal.

Our new principal was Mary Mannheim, who was a woman with a great deal of integrity, and was a natural leader. Miss Mannheim, and educator extraordinaire, brought a great deal of honor to the school and remained at Sukiran administering the educational program for several years.

It wasn't the first time that I saw the girl that defined the very essence of beauty and class. During the weekends, I'd go into Naha for a beer at one of my favorite bars, and then have dinner at one of the eating establishments. While enjoying my evening meal, I couldn't help but notice a young woman who had just entered the restaurant to join her friends. Seeing her left me with somewhat confused because I didn't know that such classy women existed on the island. She was extremely beautiful, sophisticated, smartly dressed, and appeared to be very independent. I was left speechless, but it didn't matter because I didn't have anyone to speak to anyway. That evening in Naha was the last time I saw her until I was introduced to her at a dinner party. Along with the other students in my Japanese language class, I went to a restaurant in Naha where the lovely young woman was invited to join us by our teacher, Takashiki-san, and another student, Captain Bob Van Riper. At the dinner, Susan Francis befriended her, and that meant that I was going to see her again. Again, I was speechless, but my brain was working as I thought of ways that I might get to know her better. In any case, I had fallen for her, and I was going to use my limited experience to capture her heart.

Chieko Kohagura was a girl just about any guy sane enough to admire intelligence, charm, and beauty would want as a wife. But any fellow certainly wasn't who she was looking for to become her husband. In fact, she wasn't searching for a husband at all. She had a couple of good jobs, owned one of the few cars on the island, had her own apartment, and was surrounded by a host of good friends. If she were looking for that someone special in her life, it would have to be a man who could tell her stories about Greek mythology, carry on conversations that both amused and entertained her, and maybe even played the saxophone. There was no doubt in my mind that I wanted the lovely young woman to be my wife.

My romance with Chieko-san was as slow as a turtle racing a sloth, and just about as exciting as watching a haircut. Putting it another way, it was nonexistent until I got some help from my friend, Susan Francis.

During the months of September and October, I tagged along with Susan and Chieko like a lamp post. I was always nearby, and I would occasionally shed some light on things, but that was about all I had going for me. Finally growing tired of not getting anywhere and threatening to self-immolate, I asked Susan for a favor. I wanted her to pretend she was ill so that I could spend some time alone with Chieko-san. The next morning, Susan called Chieko at her office and invited her out to the base with plans to go to the Top of the Rock Officers Club that evening. It was six o'clock when Chieko came out to her BOQ, and after the usual greetings, Susan feigned the headache of her life. Although it was part of my plan to be alone with Chieko, she was so good at acting out the part that it was difficult to believe that she really didn't have a headache.

"Chieko-san, my head is really killing me," she moaned. "Why don't you and Harvey go up to the club. I'll join you two later if I feel a little better?"

"Then I must stay here and take care of you," Chieko answered.

I hadn't figured on her compassion, so I repeated Susan's offer. "Susan said that she would join us later if she felt better, so why don't we go up to the club and have some dinner? If she doesn't feel better, since you are coming back to the BOQ anyway, you will be able to take care of her."

"All right," she finally agreed, "we will go to the club, but only for a little while."

The Top of the Rock was really swinging that night. The band was rocking, the singers were mostly in key, and the Greek tales flowed like honey from my lips. We danced, ate, and talked throughout the evening, while I tried to impress her with as much wit and charm as I could muster.

My efforts paid off, and now I was courting Chieko-san. We traveled around the island's various historical sites and its magnificent scenery. The Himeyuri Monument, Itoman, Mabuni Hill, Shuri, Onna Point, Nago, and several other places on the island. All of this was possible because Charlie let me borrow his four-door Plymouth sedan while he was out in the field.

Through the window of Charlie's freshly waxed black and white Plymouth, Chieko-san and I observed some fishermen wading through the shallow waters of the East China Sea. The sun-baked fishermen, wearing long kimonos woven from banana tree fibers, added a serene touch to a perfect fall day. Hoping to keep their garments dry, the fishermen stuffed the right side of their kimonos into their rope obis while going about the business of sweeping the sea with small fishing nets. As we approached the outer limits of the sleepy village of *Tancha,* I noticed several female rear ends protruding from among the rice paddies.

"Should we be insulted or what?" I said. "Chieko, I think we have just been mooned by those ladies."

"No, Harvey-san, there is no other way that rice can be harvested."

Suddenly, we felt a thump coming from one of the tires. "I'll be damned. I think we have a flat tire," I cried.

We got out of the car and watched as the last of the air escape from the right rear tire. The deflated tire melted into the asphalt like chocolate ice cream in the July sun.

"Don't worry, Chieko-san, I'll have it fixed in no time," I promised.

While in the process of changing the flat, an audience of villagers gathered to watch me. After I put on the spare tire, I tightened the bolts. It was then that I noticed that the spare tire was as flat as a pancake.

"Now what do we do?" I asked my girlfriend.

Out of nowhere, an elderly gentleman appeared holding a rusty tire pump. He bent over and attached the device to the now flat spare tire. And just like that, the tire began to inflate. And a minute later, the tire was full of air and we were ready hit the road.

The vigorous old guy, with the help of that corroded air pump, inflated the pride of the vanquished villagers and everybody cheered while several men shook hands with me.

With no more heroics to be performed that day, the smiling villagers of *Tancha* bid us a fond farewell.

The Marriage Ceremony

After two months of going to the Harborview Club to drink, eat, and dance, I decided that it was time we got married. Besides, the late nights where wearing on me and I needed to get some sleep. But most of all, I was madly in love with Chieko.

Christmas trees were going up everywhere and the holiday spirit was in the air when I phoned Chieko-san at the Radio Corporation of America/Ryukyu International Telephone Service office, to ask her to marry me.

"What did you say?" At first, she did not believe what she just heard.

"I said, would you marry me next Tuesday.

"This is really kind of sudden," she replied.

"You know that I love you. And I think that you love me. So let's get married." I hoped that she wouldn't come to her senses and turn me down

She was silent for a moment then she finally said the magic words. "All right, I will marry you."

"You know, you've just made me a very happy man! Now, the first thing we have to do is get two people to witness our marriage. I think I can get Charlie Higa."

"I will try to get my boss at US Airlines, Mikel Bautista," Chieko-san replied.

The following Tuesday, the four of us were at the American Consulate for the marriage ceremony. I wasn't sure what a civil ceremony was like, but it was our wedding day so I had great expectations. Charlie came in from the field and changed out of his fatigues and into a sports jacket and slacks. Mikel Bautista was wearing a business suit, and Chieko looked stunning in her white outfit. I wore a brown-stripped suit that I had purchased at Brooks Brothers in New York.

As the ceremony progressed, everything was going well until the Counselor General asked Chieko something that instantly brought out the worst in me.

"Have you ever been, or are you currently engaged in prostitution?"

Higa-san put his hand on my shoulder to keep me from losing my cool. It did some good, but I was still mad as hell. I answered the question for Chieko-san. "No. Has YOUR wife ever been a prostitute?"

"Look. I'm sorry for asking that question. Sometimes, our young GI's marry prostitutes. By the way, I'll answer your question. No, my wife has never been a prostitute," he replied.

Everyone smiled, and the rest of the marriage ceremony went off as smooth as a baby's butt.

After going to the mayor's office to pay seventeen cents for the Japanese marriage certificate, Mikel declared us legally married by exclaiming, "You are married, boy!" That comment officially marked the end of the ceremony. My bride and I went to the apartment with Higa-san so that he could change back into his fatigues. After Chieko and I asked him to bless our marriage, he did so with the skill and grace of a Lutheran minister. After we left the apartment, Charlie drove us to the middle of the city where the two of us walked up and down Kokusai Street for a couple of hours. While strolling around in the middle of Naha, we had our picture taken, stopped for a couple cups of brew at the *Mon* coffee shop, and had a pleasant dinner at the Harborview Club. Following dinner, we went to the Daiichi Hotel for remainder of the evening.

Our Apartment

The next morning, while the taxi was waiting for Chieko to take her to her office, it occurred to me that we didn't have any place to meet after work. My first thought was that maybe I'd never see her again, but my second thought was far more practical.

"Let's meet at my BOQ. We'll figure out what we are going to do from there," I said.

"All right," she replied. "I'll see you at your place," she smiled and waved goodbye as she got into her cab.

After Chieko-san left for work, I looked for another taxi to take me to Sukiran Elementary School.

That evening, Chieko came out to my BOQ, and since her roommate wasn't moving out of the apartment until the end of the month, we decided to stay at my place until then. For the time being, only Susan Francis, Mikel Bautista, and Charlie Higa knew that we were married, and things would have to remain that way until we moved into our Naha apartment. Anyway, shacking up in the BOQ with a beautiful Japanese girl was perfectly acceptable. In fact, the commanders of the various units gave a wink and a nod to those fortunate few who did so.

At the end of the month Chieko's roommate vacated the apartment and we moved from my BOQ to our place in Naha. There were two rooms and a bathroom without a door, so a guy couldn't get any privacy during those delicate times when he needed it. My wife cooked up some great meals in the tiny kitchen, and the bedroom was so small that you had to step outside to change your mind. Resting against the wall was a bed with a wooden fruit box propped underneath it to hold up the middle of the swayed back mattress. Inside the bedroom wall, a mouse visited us nightly, until one Saturday morning when I patiently waited, like a big game hunter, for two hours for the rodent to come out of his hiding place. Finally it came from the kitchen and rounded the corner into our bedroom, and when it did, I quickly put the wastebasket over the damned thing. A couple of seconds later, I opened it slightly so the mouse could stick his head out of the opening, and that was when I pounded the top of the basket and broke the mouse's neck. Now, we could finally get some sleep.

Chieko-san's father came to the *Wakamatsu* part of town to attend a business meeting, so he decided to drop by the apartment to see Chieko. But her father was in for the surprise of his life. Marrying an American was against the rules of the family, so Chieko hadn't told her father that we were married. The poor man was shocked when Chieko introduced me as her husband.

"Huh!" He responded.

After she invited her father into the apartment, I turned off the Dave Brubeck record while Chieko-san went next door to buy some *sashimi*. A few minutes later, we ate the plate of *sashimi* and rice while we engaged in occasional small talk. Chieko-san retreated to the bedroom for a few moments while her father contemplated the thought of my being his son-in-law. After that uncomfortable afternoon, we really didn't see much of her father until Mitchell was born.

When spring arrived, because the apartment was directly above a bathhouse, it became a bit toasty inside the place, so we moved to another apartment on the other side of town, just around the corner from the Harborview Club. The kitchen, living room, dining room, and bathroom were larger and more modern than our last place. And the new apartment even came with a bathroom door!

Keeping up with the habits from our dating days, we went to the Harborview Club to enjoy a steak dinner for a couple of bucks, dance to a thirteen piece band, and listen to Joe O'Toole, the club's manager, sing, "Chicago". We continued to get a big kick out of his attempts, and he gave it his best, but he didn't sound like Frank Sinatra, or even Frankie Yankovitch. Nevertheless, he was entertaining. Joe's girlfriend was a Filipina beauty whose rendition of "The Girl From Ipanema", with her soft and smooth voice, sounded a great deal like Astrud Gilberto. The bandleader knew that I was from New York, and like some big city gangster, every time we walked into the place, they stopped what they were playing and switched to "Autumn In New York".

While living in our new apartment, I took up the sport of judo. Every evening, before going to the *dojo* in Naha, I would run a couple of miles through the unpaved streets of the town to warm up for my lessons. When I started studying judo, as a test of my resolve and character, they had me practice hitting the tatami and rolling for a month of evenings. The routine continued until a black belt named Matsuda-san, took me by the arm and led me onto the *dojo* to begin my training program. I progressed rapidly, and within a few months, I had earned a brown belt, and was well on my way to a black belt.

A Trip To Edo

Springtime was in the air when Chieko and I decided to take a trip to Tokyo, the city formerly known as *Edo*. History tells us that it has been Japan's capital city since 1603, and it had the *Somei-Yoshino* or cherry blossoms as its national flower. After arriving in Tachikawa Air Base by a C-130, we took a train to Tokyo. Besides a hundred other folks on the train, there was an elderly Caucasian gentleman wearing a Frank Buck outfit complete with a sun helmet and short khaki pants. I edged my way up to the old fellow in order to strike up a conversation. The man was at about eighty-five years old and he was traveling around Japan by himself. His wife told him that she didn't want to travel because someone had to take care of the garden. When I asked him where he was from, he replied, "Altoona, Pennsylvania."

Tokyo's cherry blossoms were in full bloom painting the grey city with a welcomed touch of color. Like graceful geishas, they brought smiles of appreciation to her citizens faces. We were fortunate to get a room at the original Imperial Hotel, an elegant and sophisticated hotel designed by the great Frank Lloyd Wright. The architect built the structure in the form of an "H" and dared any earthquake to destroy it. On September 1, 1923, the great *Kanto* earthquake struck Tokyo. Although it smashed the rest of the city and killed 143,000 people, its tremors failed to damage the Imperial Hotel. In the year 1963, it was comforting to be safely tucked away in that beautiful and impregnable structure.

On our second night at the Imperial Hotel, we decided to go to a nightclub to see a floor show. We climbed into a taxi and told the cabby what we had in mind for the evening. The driver offered a few suggestions and we decided on a club in Yokohama. Arriving thirty minutes later, we pulled up in front of a nightclub where a cast of a dozen actors and singers were performing. Walking up a long flight of steps, we entered the nightclub then we were led to a table on the third floor of the nightclub. After we ordered our drinks, the next show began. Never had I ever seen anything like it before or since. The stage was on multi-levels that moved up and down with each scene change. The scenery varied from ships and horses to a picturesque countryside. Both the acting and the dancing were outstanding, and the singers were incredible.

After the show, we caught a cab back to the Imperial Hotel for a good night's sleep. The next morning we took a C-130 back to Okinawa.

At the judo class, because I had taken a week off to go on our vacation, when it was my opponents turn to practice throwing me, my timing was slightly off when he threw me over his shoulder. I didn't fall correctly and I ended up with a painful back injury that brought an end to my judo career.

Naha Elementary School

Chieko was pregnant and visits to Camp Kue Army hospital were written into our monthly schedule. Earlier that year, 1963, I moved from Sukiran Elementary to Naha Elementary School to teach sixth grade. The school was a series of Quonset huts joined by a dirt road that ran up the middle of the row of corrugated tin buildings. Just before the opening of the school year, the teachers unstacked the desks that were piled up to the ceiling and arranged them into rows. But not before we before we swept out our dust covered classrooms.

Once school began, between the F-100's taking off and landing, we taught our kids with enthusiasm and professionalism. As the year progressed, I learned that some of my students had never been outside the base, so I decided to take them on a field trip into Naha to see the market and some of the city. All of the students really enjoyed seeing the wonderful sites, and it was an excellent educational experience for everyone.

Although we had very little support from the Overseas Schools, none of the teachers complained about the lack of supplies or equipment. Ralph Estep, our principal, would go hat in hand to the various military units and asked for whatever supplies he could get. One of his major accomplishments was acquiring a broken mimeograph machine from one of the air force units that an Okinawan guy repaired for us.

Nine months passed as slowly as molasses in an ice storm, but it was finally time for Chieko-san to go to the hospital to deliver our baby. After eight hours in labor, our son was born. Mitchell Kiyoshi was very cute kid with exactly the right number of fingers and toes. After Mitchell was born, things changed for our family. Whenever we went to visit our parents in Nakadomari, grandfather and Mitchell were like two peas in a pod. In other words, they were inseparable.

The Case Of The Inside Out Undershorts

Odd things sometimes happen to strange people. Just two doors away, in the same apartment complex, lived another American who was also married to a Japanese woman. Unfortunately, she was not sophisticated with many of the modern contraptions that were in use at the time. For example, his wife sometimes bathed in the washing machine. Without judging her, I granted her the right to clean herself whatever way she wanted. Her husband, Tony, fancied himself to be a man about town who often enjoyed the company of other women. When not studying judo at the same *dojo* as I did, he would visit the bars and clubs around the town and partake in all the delicacies made available to him.

One afternoon, he returned home, and while changing his trousers, his wife noticed that his underpants were turned inside out.

"Why you underpants inside out? This morning they right way!" She exclaimed.

Tony was speechless, but his wife wasn't. She'd fussed and fumed, then she threw him out of the house. A week later, he was finally allowed back into their apartment.

Kyoto

Leaving Mitchell with Connie and Charlie Higa, we took a four-day vacation to mainland Japan. Boarding the C-130 at Naha Air Base, we struck up a conversation with a young naval officer on his way to Yokosuka. When the lunch boxes containing fried chicken were distributed to the passengers, we passed on the lunch. I recommended to the ensign that he should also forget about the fried chicken.

"You know if it gets rough up there, you might be sorry you ate that fried chicken," I said.

"Hey, I've got a cast iron stomach. It's not going to bother me," he replied.

Halfway through the flight, we hit a storm, and up came the ensign's fried chicken. The flight crew improvised a canvass booth, placed a bucket in it, and scattered newspapers on the floor for the young officer. Now safely tucked away so that no one could see him, he threw up for the remainder of the flight.

From Tachikawa Air Base, we took a long train ride to Kyoto where we spent a good part of the time sitting on the floor with newspapers under our butts, just like the other people who didn't have seats. Eventually, enough people got off the train, and the rest of us occupied the vacated seats.

While in the snow-covered city of Kyoto, we visited *Kinkaku-ji, To-ji, Shimogano* Shrine, and a host of other interesting places. We stayed in an old inn that featured a large bath area next to our tatami room. At evening time, we took our hot baths while sipping small cups of warm sake, and when it was bedtime, the two of us climbed under our futon and slept through the night like a couple of hibernating bears.

The following afternoon, we went to a small restaurant and ordered *kamameishi*, which is a small dish of chicken, peas, and rice. Although it was delicious, the meal had a price tag of twenty dollars, which was a lot of money in those days. But I dug deep into my wallet and came up with the cash to pay the bill. While eating at the restaurant, I noticed the name GETZ, written in hiragana on one of the ceiling lanterns. It was William Goetz, the producer of "*Sayonara*". The cast and crew had eaten there during the filming of that great movie.

A Fond Farewell

It was 23 November 1963, and it was a Saturday morning when we awakened by our son Yukihiro. He had come all the way from Nakadomari with a newspaper in his hand to inform us that John F. Kennedy had been assassinated. At first, I did not believe the poorly printed edition, so I got dressed and went outside to see if anyone had heard the news of the shooting of our president. From the sad looks on everybody's faces, I knew that our leader was dead. The following Monday, the schools were closed so that everyone could attend a memorial ceremony where the honor guards were Special Forces soldiers. It was an extremely sad occasion, and it was a time for all of us to thank the late President Kennedy for the many great things that he had done for our country.

Okinawa was an incredible place, I had made lifelong friends, found the love of my life, had a baby boy, studied judo, saw a good deal of mainland Japan, and enjoyed my work, but it was time to explore other new and exciting places. After receiving a transfer that spring, we prepared to leave our beloved island. Packing up our household goods and saying goodbye to our family and friends was difficult, but we were going to a new adventure in the German city of Kaiserslautern.

"I am afraid that I'm not going to able to fly back to the United States," I said to the personnel director who was busily shuffling paper over to the other side of his desk.

"And why not?" Asked the director of personnel.

"Because I am afraid to fly," I answered. "To be honest, flying scares the hell out of me. That is why I want my family and I to go to the states on the USNS *Sultan*. It's a safe ship, and I am not worried about it sinking or anything like that. Besides, the accommodations and food are excellent."

"Mr. Getz," the personnel director stopped shifting his papers and looked up at me, "our ships are being used to transport troops and supplies to Viet Nam. How about if we send you and your family with first class tickets back to the United States?"

"Well, that would be all right. Except that no matter what class we were flying, I'd still be afraid."

The director was pondering over the matter when I interjected, "that ship pulls into Okinawa once a month, and we want to be on it!"

Two days later, I received the word from headquarter that my "fear of flying" paid off, and we were scheduled to sail back to the United States on the USNS *Sultan*.

At the pier in Naha, the same place where Susan, Ruth, and I met Mr. Thomas two years earlier, we were saying our goodbyes to some of our friends and relatives. After being shown to our cabin by a crew member, we quickly made our way back up to the deck to bid a fond farewell to Charlie, Connie, and to Chieko's family. Certain that someday we would return, Chieko's mother didn't appear to be too upset about her leaving the fold. As we were slowly pulled out of the port, her parents held onto one end of the crepe ribbon while we grasped the other end of the streamer. Distance had finally broken the brightly colored strip, and we were on our way to America.

A Stopover In Korea

On the way to the states, our ship pulled into Korea for a six-hour stopover. In the harbor, like the invading GI's in the Korean War, we climbed aboard a landing craft and chugged into port to take a quick tour of the city. In the verdant Korean hills, we could see a scattering of wooden houses and small apartment buildings. After we landed at the port, we climbed out of the troop carrying boat then we walked a block before catching a bus to the center of the city. Standing on the bus, I noticed a nasty odor that smelled like a refrigerator full of spoiled food. I checked Mitchell's diaper, but it was clean. Then I examined the bottom of my shoes and found nothing but leather and rubber. I also looked at Chieko's shoes, but came up with same thing. Finally, after exhausting all possibilities, I realized the source of that god-awful smell. It was their national treat, *kim chee,* a highly spiced pickled cabbage buried in the ground for a few months then dug back up and eaten by the Koreans. Everybody had consumed tons of the stuff, and the longer we were on the bus, the more we smelled it.

After riding around the town for a while, we got off the bus and walked the narrow streets of Inchon. At the time, the city was mostly dotted with restaurants, small shops, and hundreds of pedestrians walking in both directions on the crowded sidewalks. Taxis and buses were the main forms of transportation, and the lingering smell of *kim chee* acted as a cloud of stench that hung over the entire town. Following a short walk around a section of the city, we returned to the port and climbed back into the landing craft and chugged back out to our ship. Eighteen days would go by until we, once again, set foot on land.

The personnel director was absolutely correct when he said that teachers were not traveling by ship anymore. As we crossed the vast sea, the boat was nearly empty. A scattering of soldiers and marines, and a small group of civilians were the only other passengers. Also onboard were four nurses with regular duty hours. We hardly saw Mitchell during our Pacific crossing because, at their request, he was in the care of the nurses most of the time. The three of us enjoyed our time together, and the trip was great except for a typhoon that lasted three days. During the storm, we spent most of the time in our cabin reading and balancing ourselves in our beds to keep from falling onto the floor.

San Francisco

After our twenty-day voyage, San Francisco was even more beautiful than I remembered it. In fact, the city named, "Baghdad-by-the-Bay" by columnist, Herb Caen, was breathtaking. Her terraced white buildings gave the city a ghostly but embracing appearance, and the magnificent Golden Gate Bridge was mysterious and inviting as it peeked out through the fog. The steep hills surrounding the town appeared to envelop the city in a valley of cable cars, buses, automobiles, streetcars, and dreams of living in such a place.

Chieko-san, who was standing on the far side of cabin, looked a bit reticent when I said, "Take a look at this view. It's really beautiful!"

I was completely surprised when she finally spoke, "No. I'm not in the mood to look at the country that destroyed my island."

Taken back by the intensity in her voice, I replied, "But the view is really great. Come here and take a look for yourself."

"No, thank you." She answered.

After pulling into the dock, the passengers bid a fond farewell to the ship as we disembarked from the USNS *Sultan*. Hailing a cab, I asked the taxi driver to take us to the Pickwick Hotel, located in the center of the city. After checking into our room, we went out for a walk on Market Street to get a good look at the town and its people. During those times, everybody dressed up when they went downtown to shop or walk around. Most of the men wore suits, coats, and fedoras. The women wore conservative dresses, hats, and gloves. Everywhere we walked, people were very pleasant to us, and they made a big fuss over Mitchell. Thankfully, this seemed to have changed Chieko's mind about Americans.

"These Americans are different from the GI's back on Okinawa. They seem to be very nice," she observed.

"Yes. They are very kind," I agreed.

For two days, we walked in and out of the city's department stores and shops, rode the trolley car, where Mitchell peed all over my green suit, toured Chinatown, Telegraph Hill, Coit Tower, Van Ness Avenue, and Japan Town. We ate at a couple of Japanese and Chinese restaurants, as well as Alioto's at Fisherman's Wharf where I, once again, listened to Fritz on the accordion, and Maria, still wearing her dirndl, sing and dance to a variety of German songs. Our two days in San Francisco were hardly enough time to see everything, but without traveling to any of the other towns in the United States, Chieko decided that it was her favorite city in America.

After taking a taxi out to the San Francisco airport, we checked our bags and sat down in the busy waiting area. We were flying to New York, then on to Altoona by train to visit my parents and relatives. While waiting in the terminal for our flight, I was surprised to see my old girlfriend, Katie McNabb. She was also waiting for a flight, probably to the East Coast. But like a true coward, although she walked past me several times, I pretended that I didn't recognize her. Instead of looking up from my newspaper to greet her and introduce my wife and child, I kept my head buried in the paper and made like I didn't recognize her. The truth was that I didn't want her to get excited about our chance meeting and then become quickly disappointed when I introduced her to my wife and son.

Chieko was amazed at the vastness of America. From her airplane window, she observed the deserts, plains, checkered farmers fields, the Rocky Mountains, and the towns and cities that made up the United States. It was during the middle of our flight that Chieko remarked that it was ridiculous that little Japan thought it could defeat a country as large as America.

After our plane landed in New York, we took a taxi from Kennedy airport into Pennsylvania Station to catch our train to Altoona. From the ticket teller, we learned that the next train to my hometown wasn't until seven o'clock in the morning, so we roamed around Manhattan and passed the time by going to a few jazz clubs and restaurants. Waitresses and jazz fans took time out of their busy night to make a fuss over our little son.

Early the next morning, after getting our tickets on a steam-driven train, the three of us took our seats and settled in for the six-hour train ride to visit with my parents.

Altoona, Pennsylvania

Other than the soot blowing out of the engine and back into our faces, our trip to Altoona went smoothly. Pulling into the Pennsylvania Railroad Station, while looking through the train window, I saw my parents standing on the wooden platform with smiles on their anxious faces. Meeting their grandson and daughter-in-law for the very first time was an exciting moment for the both of them. Looking at their happy faces, I knew that everything was going to be just fine.

After we embraced, I presented Chieko and Mitchell. "Mom and Dad, I'd like you to meet my wife, Chieko, and your grandson, Mitchell."

Mother smiled and gave Chieko a big hug then looked over at Mitchell, "Now let's see that little boy of ours. Pooie! I think he's got a load in his pants. Let's go into the building and change him," Mother laughed.

While in Altoona, we visited with my uncles and aunts and they all were very kind and showed feelings of love for the newest members of our family. My Uncle Lou held Chieko's hand when he spoke to her, and for the first time in my life, I saw him as a warm and loving man. Lou Karp was a soldier in the battle of Okinawa, so he knew exactly what Chieko had endured. Uncle Lou told us a couple of stories that I found quite interesting, including the deaths of Ernie Pyle and Leo Kaplan. He also related another tale of the gentleman in a white kimono.

I was lying in a ditch protecting myself from enemy fire when I heard the shot that killed Ernie Pyle. A sniper shot him just as Ernie stuck his head up to look around. He shouldn't have done that. Later, I saw his body before they carried him away.

When I was on the ship taking us to Okinawa, I was made a gunner because of my previous flight training. You see, I could identify most of the Japanese planes, so the chances of my shooting down an American plane were slim. During the day, it was pretty boring, but when the sun set, the kamikaze planes attacked with the setting sun behind them. I think I was responsible for shooting down one of their planes. One day, I was on the ship when a kamikaze crashed into us. I was thrown into the sea, and after treading water for a hour or so, I was rescued by another Jewish fellow from Pittsburgh, Pennsylvania. Anyway, Leo Kaplan was his name, and I'll always be grateful to him. A few hours after rescuing me, Leo Kaplan was killed. After the war, I went to visit his parents in Pittsburgh, where his father drove a taxi. I went to the cab company's office to find him. His boss called for him, and after hearing my story, Mr. Kaplan asked me to come to his house to meet his wife. Leo's mother cried in my arms after I told her what her son had done for me.

A few days after the Japanese surrender, my friend and I were out walking near the Tenth Army headquarters, when we came upon an old man wearing a completely white kimono. Standing in front of us with a broad smile on his bearded and aging face, in perfect English, he invited us to his hut for a cup of tea. While there, we sipped green tea and talked about ourselves, and our lives in America. I'll always remember him as a very kind man.

During my final summer in Altoona, I studied German for three to four hours every day at the local Penn State library. After finishing for the day, I would go home and practice on my Yiddish speaking mother. With her help, I learned a great deal of German as I prepared to move to that country.

Although mother had lived all of her life in Altoona, there was no longer any reason to remain there; several of our relatives had already moved to the west coast of the United States. They were moving to Los Angeles, and there was no debate on the subject. Dad would have preferred to remain in Altoona, but he had no choice in the matter. It was goodbye to all of his customers in western Pennsylvania, and to the Sky Brothers Frozen Food Corporation.

My uncle Sam and aunt Ann had already moved to the Los Angeles area and my parents were soon going to join them. Uncle Sam continued with his shoe store business, but in the back of his mind, the war had created a plethora of experiences. While most men were reluctant to talk about their part in the battles they fought, my Uncle Sam told me a story about North Africa.

There was sand everywhere. It was in our food, our clothes, our eyes, and in our weapons. I knew that the desert was going to kill me if I didn't get a transfer. I wrote my former colonel in desperate hope that he would get me out of there. He wrote back to tell me that he was getting me transferred to his headquarters in Cairo. Now, I hate sand so much that ever since the war, I have never even gone to a beach.

On the way to catch our plane to Germany, we stopped in New York to see my brother and my sister-in-law, Sandy. The World's Fair was in New York, so we went there a couple of days before he driving us to McGuire Air Force Base in New Jersey. After arriving at the airfield, we saw that there were a few 707 jets on the runway and I was certain that one of them was our airplane.

"One thing about the Overseas Schools, we travel first class." I remarked to Lou.

Always a skeptic, Lou replied, "Well, I hope you are right."

About thirty minutes later, all three Boeing 707s had departed leaving an old propeller driven DC-3 that had been hiding between the now departed jets. We learned that it was the plane that was going to take us across the Atlantic Ocean.

Masking my disappointment, we bid goodbye to Lou and Sandy, then climbed aboard the aging aircraft to find our seats. After boarding the propellor-driven aircraft, we were told by the flight attendant that it was the last flight for the DC-3, and from then on, 707s would carry passengers to Germany. Somehow, that didn't make me feel any better about the flight.

Europe

It was uninvitingly cold and dark when we landed for a brief stopover in Greenland, but we had enough time to go to the snack bar for a couple of burgers and cokes. After we finished our sandwiches, we re-boarded the airplane and took off into the dark sky. Somewhere in the middle of the Atlantic Ocean, a few religious passengers in the back of the plane began singing Christian hymns. However, after some of the other people on the plane loudly complained, mercifully, they stopped.

Arriving in Frankfurt in the late afternoon, we were bused to a BOQ in the center of the town for a good night's rest. Before our group broke up for the evening, we were told to report the next morning to the replacement depot to receive our school assignments. I knew we were going to Kaiserslautern, so I didn't give it much thought. What I did think about was that the Germans had been the perpetrator of the worst crimes in the long and tragic history of the Jews.

Mitchell was crying and he was as hungry as a lion cub. So I told Chieko that I'd go out to find some milk for the little guy. Outside the BOQ, it was evilly dark, and a slight drizzle fell from the moonless sky. Only an hour earlier, cars raced up and down the streets of Frankfurt with impunity, and the once busy sidewalks that had been occupied by hundreds of faceless Germans a short time ago, were now abandoned to the loneliness of the night. Walking down a side street, I thought about the Holocaust, and if it had been nineteen years earlier, this Jew would be running for his bloody life and I imagined the pursuing Nazis chasing after me with their weapons blazing away. It was at that moment that I broke out into a run leaving my clothes saturated with a cold sweat. Along the roadside, gargantuan trees grew even more immense as their branches reached out to trap me in their gigantic limbs. Situated on both sides of the street were harsh concrete edifices that pressed inward as they tried to squeeze me between their towering structures. The numerous shrubs scattered along the curb tried like hell to trip up my fleeing legs, and the spirits of the millions of Jews who lost their lives to Hitler's murderers, transformed the dismal night into a black hole from which there was no escape. For a few moments, I was in another time--but not another place. Deep within the bowels of the blood soaked earth, the evil Teutonic gods were laughing at me. About to scream for mercy, I came upon a grocery store and ran inside the shop for protection. Or was it retribution? I had the look of fear on my face and revenge in my heart. The proprietor cast his beady eyes on me in a very odd way, but his calm but confused gaze somehow settled me down. Suddenly, I remembered why I was there. "*Eine flashe milch, bitte.*" I had recovered my senses and asked for a bottle of milk. The German, wary of my presence, left the counter and walked back to the cooler to fetch the milk. After paying the gentleman, I ran back to our room without telling Chieko about my depressing encounter.

The panic that I experienced that night was the result of reoccurring dreams that I had throughout my teenage years. In those dreams, Nazis were chasing me down the street hell-bent on killing me and then throwing my body into an oven. After my death, they would toss my ashes into a trench to become part of the German soil for time immemorial. In any event, the nightmare hadn't come true, and it was my first and last panic attack in Germany.

The next morning, we reported to the replacement depot, a large and mostly vacant room with a few metal desks and chairs scattered about the place. A large group of people milled about and talked to one another while waiting for their names to be called. Finally, it was my turn to be summoned to the front to the front of the room to receive my assignment. It was Landstuhl, a small post about ten miles from Kaiserslautern. At first, I tried to change my posting because I was supposed to be going to Kaiserslautern, not Landstuhl. However, my seemingly persuasive, but futile efforts fell on deaf ears. After everybody received their assignments, those of us going to Kaiserslautern, Landstuhl, Ramstein, and Pirmasens, boarded a military bus and traveled up the autobahn to our destinations. Once we arrived in Landstuhl, Chieko and I were happy that we weren't going to Kaiserslautern. Our first glance at the place revealed that it was a very nice but small post that sat on top of very steep hill. The Army hospital, the *raison d'etre* for the base, was near the main gate, while the housing area was located across the road behind a copse of evergreen trees.

After checking into our BOQ room, I walked a half mile down the hill to buy a couple of Parkbrau beers at a German supermarket. Later that day, I drank my first German beer, and because I wasn't used it, I came up with a king-sized headache. On the second day, I had the other beer, but this time, I didn't get a hangover. Ten days later, I bought a red, four-seater Triumph convertible, and we were off to the nearby Ramstein Air Force Base to do some shopping, as well as to the Kaiserslautern, Pirmasens, and Zweibrucken post exchanges.

We stayed in the BOQ for a couple of weeks before moving to an on-base temporary apartment. Two months later, we settled into a permanent apartment where we did our best to establish ourselves as good neighbors.

A plump, but energetic woman, who spoke a little English, was my German language teacher. She used the magazine approach to teaching, and it worked pretty well with me. The serious but patient Frau, had a collection of magazines that I would translate from German to English. I went to her house every Tuesday for my lessons, but three months later, she told me that I didn't need to come anymore. It seemed that I knew everything about the language that a guy needed to know in order to get around in Germany.

"I can't teach you anymore German. You already know everything!" The big woman declared.

My first principal at Landstuhl Elementary School was Ron Herbert, but he left at the end of the year and was replaced by the diminutive Ed McNalley. The new principal sat in a desk that was much too large for the little fellow who seemed lost in a forest of oak. But Mr. McNalley was a decent principal simply because he permitted the teachers to teach their classes with no interference from the administration.

Colonel Prescott, a psychiatrist at the Army hospital, came to my combination class of fifth and sixth graders once a week to observe my teaching methods for a book he was writing. About a year later, I got a letter from my brother, Allen, who was teaching in Provo, Utah at the time. While in the teachers room, he picked up the book that Colonel Prescott had authored, and he saw my name on the inside cover page. Allen was excited that his brother was being used as a model for other teachers to emulate.

At the end of the year, I transferred to Landstuhl Junior High School where George Gunderson, an excellent administrator and musician, served as the principal. Much to my regret, a year later, Betty Johnson became the school's leader. But we shall hear more about her later in the story.

During the Easter vacation, we took a trip to Amsterdam to enjoy the tulips and roam around that exciting and historic megalopolis. Deciding to try camping for the first time for the simple reason that we needed to be parsimonious, I drove to the camp site in the former Olympic stadium. After we found a spot to call our own, I decided to set up my tent in record time. With the very curious, but much slower Germans and Dutch campers watching me, I ran around the tent pounding the pegs into the ground as fast as my skinny legs could carry me. The clearly jealous international spectators were shaking their collective heads as I went about the business of settling into the space that was given to me. However, I recognized tent envy when I saw it! After I got the last peg in the ground, I realized that something was wrong. I couldn't get under the tent to put the pole where it belonged, which happened to be in the middle of the tent. In my rush to assemble the tent, I had nailed the canvass tent to the ground. At that point, the once envious campers were laughing their fat butts off while I pulled the pegs out and started again. This time, I got it right.

That night, the weather changed for the worse. Snow blanketed the entire campsite and the temperature dipped down into the teens turning the tent into an icebox. The following morning, I tried starting the stove, but I couldn't get the damn thing to work. That is when I remembered that our friends, Cathy and Marvin Dwyer had arrived at the campsite overnight. I walked out onto the snow-covered grounds and began my search for the experienced campers. If I found them, Marvin could probably get the heater started. After looking at the tents for about five minutes, I finally found their tent. It was still early in the morning and they might not answer if they knew it was me. Fancying myself a master of voice disguises, I decided that my best bet was to imitate a German. *Gut Mogen. ist der mann da?* I heard some rumbling inside the tent as the two of them got out of their sleeping bags to see who was calling for them. Marvin peeled open the door of his tent and came face to face with yours truly. "Oh no! It's Getz. What do you want?" Resuming my normal voice, I explained that I couldn't get the stove started and that perhaps he could help me to get it going. We walked over to my tent containing the two human popsicles, and after a great deal of pumping, Marv got the heater started.

The next day, we decided that we had enough of camping for a while, so we moved to a warm motel with a cozy bed and a heated bathroom.

While in Amsterdam, we visited Ann Frank's house, the old synagogue, the Van Gogh museum, the Rijksmuseum, the outdoor market, and traveled to the outskirts of town to see the windmills and beautiful tulips. We saw hundreds of ridiculously narrow buildings built along the Prinsengracht, Keizegracht, and Herengracht canals as we walked over its many small bridges.

Amsterdam was the home of some famous people, including the Jewish philosopher, Baruch Spinoza (1632-1677). He lived in the Portuguese section of the city, and was famous for his published efforts. After his philosophy was studied by thousands of intellects, Spinoza was expelled from the Amsterdam synagogue for filing suit in a civil court rather than with the synagogue authorities.

Another fellow that was hard to overlook was the painter, Vincent Van Gogh (1853-1890). The mad artist was a post-impressionist who cut off his left ear and gave it to a prostitute with instructions to guard it carefully.

The Netherlands was a beautiful and captivating country, and we promised ourselves that we would return to the land of canals, windmills and bridges. On our way back to Germany, we stopped in Arnhem to see where American, British, and Polish paratroopers fought their way through the city only to be defeated by the Germans. While there, I went into a meat store to get some salami and bread for a picnic. When I spoke German to the woman who was behind the counter, she reprimanded me. "Do not speak German in here. You may speak French, Dutch, or English, but do not speak German."

It was about that time that our son, Yukihiro, who had been living with his grandparents, came from Okinawa to be part of our family. It wasn't long before he made several friends, and he soon spoke English almost like an American. Being that the city was only an hour and a half away, our first trip with Yuki was to Luxembourg. While there, we had lunch and wandered around inside the walls of the town. Like most teenagers, Yuki was introspective, but kind and all the way through junior and senior high school, he kept up with his grades while participating in soccer and track.

With help from the MWR (Morale, Welfare, and Recreation), I took up photography and furniture making at the base hobby shop. My carpentry instructor was a very talented fellow named Ron Black, an Afro-American, who was an accomplished painter and carpenter extraordinaire. During his lessons, the former army captain's style was a bit overbearing, but it was certainly instructive. Under his strict guidance, I sanded a certain way, cut another way, and stained with panache. Once the lessons were over for the night, he invited me to his office for a couple of glasses of rum and coke, and to listen to his Miles Davis records. There were those times when the artist would invite us to his apartment in Kaiserslautern where scores of painting lined the walls, while dozens more were stacked in his studio. He once had a one-man show in New York City, but he stubbornly refused to sell his "babies." On several weekends, Ron Jackson and his Polish girlfriend came to our house for a night of *sukiyaki*. After we finished our dinner, the four of us stayed up until the wee hours of the morning listening to my tapes of Miles Davis and John Coltrane.

Taking photographs had interested me for quite some time, so I decided to seriously pursue the art form. It wasn't long before I became a dark room rat at the base photo lab that was located next to Ron's hobby shop. Under the tutorage of Hans the photographer, I learned to develop film, print, enlarge, and use my Nikon F. Hans always replied in the same way whenever I'd come up with a good photograph, "Vhat you vant? Eggs in your bier!"

I was shooting portraits of kids in natural settings and men flying around in helicopters when I took a flight in Captain Prescott's chopper. The veteran pilot warned me that if the damn thing crashed, and I was still alive, I was to run like hell because civilians weren't allowed to go on joy rides. We circled the town of Landstuhl taking pictures, including shots of the town's famous Bismarck Tower, several farms, and the nearby forest. About a half hour into the flight, while looking through the lens of my camera at the sights below, I became nauseous and began praying that the pilot would get a call to go on a mission somewhere. My prayers were soon answered. About two miles from home, in the forest surrounding Landstuhl Army Medical Center, Prescott received a call that an accident had occurred on the autobahn and that his assistance was needed immediately. The pilot landed his helicopter in the forest and I jumped out and hiked back to our apartment.

The chopper that I flew in, just a week later, crashed and burned. Fortunately, the pilot and his passengers, all friends of mine, ran like hell from the burning chopper and no one was injured.

A year earlier, Captain Prescott had the dubious distinction of being the first helicopter pilot wounded in the Viet Nam War. He had been shot in the leg, and those wounds kept him in the hospital for a couple of weeks.

Chieko was pregnant, and it was time for the little one to wiggle out of his or her womb and enter the world of the living. After putting on her make up and dressing warmly, we tramped across the snowy, tree-lined field. Perhaps it was a bit foolish, but it was only a block away so we decided that walking to the hospital wasn't such a bad idea. Upon our arrival, the nurses took Chieko into the labor room while I grabbed a seat in the lobby to prepare for the long wait. A few minutes later, a nurse walked by with a bundle of laundry. I stopped her and asked, "Is everything going OK in the delivery room?" She smiled and pulled back one of the green sheets. Wrapped in the starched linen was our baby daughter, Michelle Yumiko.

An unlikely acquaintance that I made during my time in Germany was Herr Krause, a complex man whose path through life, especially that of a one-time soldier, remains an enigma to me. After several months of stories during our visits with Herr Krause and his wife in Kaiserslautern, I finally pieced together a partial picture of the man. Before the war, he attended a seminary to become a protestant minister, and while studying at the school, he learned to speak Hebrew. When the war broke out, he joined the *Wehrmacht* to fight against the Russians on the eastern front. It was during that time that he became a member of the infamous *Schutzsaffle,* otherwise known as the SS. According to Herr Krause, he wasn't a member of the organization for very long because he didn't have the right stuff to be an SS soldier.

While still a member of the notorious SS, he told this story to us.

My friend and I were walking down the street in the town of Auschwitz. We had just come out of a coffee shop when something very strange occurred. It was snowing like crazy, and everything was covered with a white blanket. But my friend and I noticed that other things were coming down with the snow. There were materials mixed with the falling snow that we didn't recognize, and there was an odd smell in the air. Since we were not allowed into the camp, we didn't know what was happening there, so I didn't give it much thought. Now, I know what it was. It was residue of burning bodies.

Herr Krause said that living under Hitler regime was not having the right to make choices, and that fear was a constant companion. One evening, while we were at his home in Kaiserslautern, he pointed out houses in the neighborhood were Jews once lived, including the grocery store on the corner. He said that he would awaken in the morning to discover that another Jewish family had been taken away, but there was nothing anybody could do about it.

"If you spoke up or asked questions, you would be gone, too," the soft-spoken German said.

One of the weaknesses that Herr Krause couldn't mask was his proclivity to admire beautiful women. When a damsel came into view, he was mesmerized by her very presence. One afternoon, he drove me into Kaiserslautern to pick up my repaired automobile, and while he was driving through the city, he stared at all the good-looking young women as they paraded by his car. It was only luck that kept him from crashing his automobile as Krause focused his beady eyes on the *hubshe frauen*.

One morning, as was my custom, I went to the teachers' room to get a cup of coffee before going on to class. I saw Herr Krause pacing back and forth like a caged tiger. And he was as grey as a mouse.

"Herr Krause, are you all right?" I first thought was that he might be having a heart attack.

At first, he could not speak. He tried to talk, but words failed him. Finally, after a minute or two, he was able to get out a sentence. "Wha... what does...who does she think I am?"

"What is the problem, Herr Krause?" I asked.

"What does she think I am?" he repeated.

Although I suspected who he was talking about, I asked, "Who is she, and what did she say to upset you?"

"She is our principal. Who does she think I am to say such a thing to me?"

Herr Krause straightened himself up to his full six-foot two inch frame, took a deep breath before adjusting his glasses. "Mrs. Johnson said to me that she guessed that Hitler hadn't killed enough of them... Jews. Who and what does she think I am?"

The Israelis had just defeated the Arabs in the 1967 war, and her comment on the victory was expressed in a way that left my German colleague visibly shaken and speechless.

"Herr Krause. If there is anything you want me to do? I'm with you all the way. If you want to file charges, I'll back you up," I offered.

He did nothing about Mrs. Johnson's indiscretion, but from that day until I left Landstuhl, I found myself wanting to strangle the woman. Every time I entered her office, after I got past the smell of her German secretary's armpits, I found my hands balling up into fists. By Jesus, I was going to murder her if I didn't get the hell out of town.

We had made several close friends while living in Germany. Marvin and Cathy Dwyer were among them. However, they left Landstuhl a year earlier for her new assignment at Letterman Hospital in San Francisco. She was a major in the Nurse Corps, and Marvin was an elementary teacher who had his sights set on becoming an episcopalian minister. Major Joe Beritto and his wife were also good friends, and so were Colonel Waters and his girlfriend, Barbara. Erika Geller was our school librarian, who always had a smile on her Aryan face, was considered a friend of ours. Then there was Gus DiAmato and his wife, a fellow with a keen sense of humor who could make a grieving widow smile. Gus was the principal of Mannheim High School, and embraced all that life afforded him.

Copenhagen, Denmark

It was during the spring break when the balding and humorous Gus DiAmato and his British wife, Alice, traveled with us to Copenhagen, a city made famous by the such folks as Victor Borge and Hans Christian Anderson. Our travel plans included rendezvousing with another couple from Oslo, Norway to partake in the wonderful food and the sites around the city. On our itinerary were the Christianborg Palace, Tivoli Gardens and the district of Nyhavn.

During our second evening in Copenhagen, Chieko and I went to a jazz club to listen to some good music. While drinking with a group of Danes, who were sitting at our table, I promised them that some of the jazzmen from that night's George Wein concert would come to the club to sit in with the house band. All they had to do was wait until midnight to get the treat of their young lives. Midnight came, and the musicians from the concert, as earlier promised, began filing into the Montmartre Jazz Club.

Clark Terry was the first musician to enter the club. He quickly took out his trumpet and started jamming with the house band. Next to enter was Bob Brookmeyer, who joined the group with his valve trombone. A few minutes later, there was a commotion at the front door. Looking over at the entrance way, I saw three guys trying to get in the door at the same time. Two of the musicians were holding up the third one. The guy they were holding up was none other than James Moody.

"Holy Jesus! That is James Moody," I said to Chieko. "Let's go over and help them get through the door. I don't think he'll remember me, but what the hell!" I said

We walked over to the door and I said, "James Moody. How are you, man?"

He looked up and said, "Getz, what the f--k are you doing here?

The next day, on our way out of the city, we decided to drive to a sandwich shop to get a bag of open-faced sandwiches (smorgasbords) to eat on the ferryboat back to Germany. After purchasing our liver delights, we returned to our car to discover that it was illegally parked in a no parking zone. Leaving the city after three days of sightseeing and walking through Tivoli Gardens was great, but the last thing we needed was a traffic ticket.

"What does it say, Harv?" Gus asked.

Dear Sir or Madam:

We hope that you enjoyed your stay in our fair city, and that you will pay us a visit again in the future. The next time you visit us, although parking may sometimes be hard to find, we hope that you will not violate our parking regulations. Again, thank you for coming to our city.

Major Joe Beritto

Major Beritto held to the *weltanschauung* that life was a series of small steps that were measured in terms of his version of reality. The sun rose in the morning, and set at night, and everything that happened in between could be somehow controlled. He had his idiosyncrasies, but for the most part, his rather simple philosophy served him well throughout his career as a soldier.

"You know, Harvey," said the balding army major, "I always report late to my new duty stations."

"Why is that, Joe?" I inquired.

"Because when I report late to my new assignment, it is always a big deal and reports have to be filed. But there is really no excuse for reporting late, and that is why things don't go well for me at first. For a few months, people keep their eyes on me just waiting for me to screw up again. But I don't. Eventually, they learn that I'm good at what I do, and they stop worrying about me. As time goes by, they say to each other, 'that major is a pretty good soldier.' I get noticed early and remain that way throughout my tour of duty."

I couldn't argue with his logic. It worked for him and that kind of thinking would later get him promoted to lieutenant colonel.

It was while we were visiting a park in nearby Saarbrucken, that Major Beritto pointed out a basic flaw in the German character.

"See the way the Germans are jammed up at the entrance of the park trying to get in before the next guy? As you can see, they aren't getting very far. I would say that the German people respond to whoever is the loudest, and in command," Joe observed.

"Watch this," he said. He walked over, or I should say, marched over to the crowd of people who were jamming their way through the turnstile. "All right, everybody line up. You are going to line up and go through this gate one person at a time."

Now, there was a sense of order and discipline as the Germans lined up instead of elbowing their way through the gate. "Now that is more like it," Major Beritto said approvingly.

Colonel Bill Waters, Joe's commanding officer, was a slightly overweight, handsome middle-aged fellow with a full head of gray hair and piercing blue eyes. With his girlfriend, Barbara, a pretty and bespectacled woman, came to our apartment on Saturday evenings to eat Japanese food and drink sake. After feasting and drinking the rice wine for a few hours, the four of us would fall asleep on the tatami mats that we brought from Okinawa. Barbara, who was our high school librarian, was very much in love with Bill, and he was also crazy about her. Although the colonel was never able to divorce his estranged wife, after he retired, the two of them spent the rest of their lives together in Virginia.

As far as German school librarians go, there was none better than Erika Geller. She worked at the elementary school keeping all the books in the Dewey Decimal System. A few years after we left Landstuhl, she married an American doctor and moved to Sacramento, California.

Barcelona, Spain

Walking around Barcelona with the tune "Besame Mucho" played by ten trombones and a rhythm section going around in my head, we had an encounter with a group of gawking Spaniards on the Rala Reial. For some odd reason, in the middle of the busy street, people were staring at us and talking among themselves. I could have passed for a Spaniard with my black hair, dark features, and mustache. Chieko looked perhaps Japanese or Chinese, and Mitchell, could have been anything. Finally, one of the men stepped forward from the rest of the group.

"What ARE you?" He asked.

"Americans," I answered. "Americans."

Running the length of the beautiful Costa Brava was a beach with a campsite where we had pitched our tent. Mitchell loved living like a homeless kid and playing in the sand for a few days. After our morning outdoor shower, we went into Barcelona to tour the capital city of Catalonia. We saw such sights as the La Rambla, Barri Gotic, the Sagrada Familia, and went to a tourist trap to see a woman, who was hoping for a big tip, painfully make her way through a Spanish dance. We also attended a bullfight, where the mighty matador slaughtered the hapless bull in front of a couple thousand screaming fans.

Two days later, we were driving back to Germany, where somewhere up in the mountains of Spain, Mitchell was enjoying himself by playing with Chieko's wedding band. That is when I noticed that the camping paraphernalia tied to the top of our car had come loose for the third time. I pulled over to the side of the road to secure the gear, but for some reason, I hesitated.

"Chieko, I'm getting awfully tired of tying this camping gear to the top of our car."

Chieko got out of the car and stared at the tent and the camping items. "Harv, to be honest, I wouldn't mind if we threw everything over the cliff," she said.

"Do you really think we should do that," I replied.

"Yes, I do," she said.

It took about twenty seconds to remove all the camping gear from the top of the car. After we separated the borrowed items that had to be returned to MWR, with a flourish, I unceremoniously threw the tent and some of the other gear over the side of the cliff. Still clanging and banging their way to the bottom of the ravine, Chieko and I had a good laugh as we climbed back into our car. We were finally free of all the stuff, and we sped away relieved that we longer had to worry about what was on top of our roof. As for the ring that Mitchell was playing with, we believe we also threw it over the cliff.

Alpbach, Austria

During our three years in Germany, we visited several counties where we enjoyed a variety of rich experiences. France, Luxembourg, the Netherlands, Austria, Spain, and Denmark all left an indelible marks on us. In Austria, I attended a six-week course on American history in the alpine village of Alpbach. It was a typical picturesque village with its wooden houses adorning flower-laden balconies, and dirndl and lederhosen clad citizens going about the business of completing their daily chores. For the first four weeks of my stay, I lived in a college dorm with the other students. At the Stanford University summer workshop, during the sessions morning lectures, I would stare out the huge window at the gigantic mountains that loomed over us instead of paying attention to the professor lecturing on American history. While screwing around in the dormitory one day, a group of us marched around the hallway with combs under our noses shouting, *Wir wollen mehr Lebensraum* (We want more living space), while looking like a parade of Hitlers. I think we scared the living crap out of the *putzfraus* (housekeepers).

Eating was a fabulous experience at the Alpbach Inn. *Mohr edama bitte,* we'd say to the waitress shortly after she served our first cheese course. All of us became gluttons and we would ask for second helpings of everything. *Mohr fleiche, bitte* (More meat, please) *Mohr karteufen bitte.* (More potatoes, please). I put on a few extra pounds with the rich, but excellent Austrian food they fed us. I tried balancing my eating by hiking in the Alps, but I guess that didn't work out very well. And to make matters worse, Chieko and Mitchell came to Alpbach for my final two weeks of the nine-credit course where we stayed in a room just above a *conditorei*, a sweet shop. After leaving Austria, it took me two months to get back to my original weight.

Augsburg, West Germany

Hitler's autobahn had come a long way since his engineers, under the leadership of Fritz Todt, had originally designed the highway. Now, it was a modern freeway system that ran across the length and width of Germany. As we were speeding along the highway, somewhere in the vicinity of Augsburg, our Triumph Herald developed engine trouble. The darn thing started clanging loudly every time it made a rotation, and the noise coming from the engine was increasing by the minute. Pulling over to the side of the roadway next to a highway phone, I called the *autobahnmeister,* Ten minutes later, he pulled up in his repair truck. After examining the engine, he declared it, *kaput!* The *autobahnmeister* said that the pistons were about to blow up through the hood if I continued to drive it. When I asked if I could make it into Augsburg, he replied, "You might, if you don't drive it too fast and let it rest once in while."

Following the mechanics recommendation, that is exactly what we did. After reaching the top of a hill, I turned off the engine and let it float until we reached the bottom of the grade. We successfully limped into Augsburg, but everything was closed because of a three-day holiday, so the repairs would have to wait until Tuesday. After carefully checking on our funds, we went to a pension for five dollars a day. The bill included breakfast and dinner.

While staying at the inn, a German sailor came into our room to chew the fat and talk about his days at sea. After speaking to the fellow for approximately forty-five minutes, I realized that I had been speaking to him in German, and I was absolutely delighted with my progress. That afternoon, we went into town to explore the city and have a bite to eat. As we walked to one of the intersections, although I didn't know why, a cold chill and the frightening feeling that somehow, I had been there before, and that gave me the creeps. I quickly turned away from the corner of the street and retreated back the same way that we had come for another cup of coffee. But somehow, the place continued to haunt me, so after finishing our coffee, we returned to the site. When we arrived at the mysterious corner, I looked up at the street sign that was mounted on a brick wall. It was called *Judenstrasse,* Jew Street. It was the site of the old Jewish ghetto.

It was now Tuesday, and after checking out a few automobile repair garages, we decided that because we didn't have the money, repairing the car wasn't an option. Having no other choice, we drove out to the Augsburg Army Base to see about buying a new car. As far as I could tell, it was the only way to get it back to Landstuhl with no money. When the salesman looked out the window of the portable building at my polished four-seater Triumph, he decided that trading in the automobile as a down payment for a new one was a pretty good deal. After some quick paperwork, we were on our way to Landstuhl in our new Volkswagon 1200.

Paris

We were on our way to the romantic city of Paris when the car's fuel gauge indicated that we were running low on gas. I pulled into an Esso station, the only oil company that accepted American military gas coupons, and waited a few minutes for the attendant to come to our car. But for some reason, there seemed to be a problem. An automobile pulled up to the next pump and was immediately given a tank of gas. Two minutes later, another customer pulled into the service station, and he was also quickly served. I began to get a little upset and wondered what the hell was going on. I had my family in the car and I didn't want any trouble. I just wanted some gasoline, and we would be back on the road to Paris.

"I'm going into the office to see what the problem is," I said to Chieko.

"All right. But don't get angry," my wife warned.

"Don't worry, I just want to find out what is happening," I said

I walked into the office but no one was there. *OK. If that is what you want, I'll just take down your name and license number and write to Esso. Let's see now, Monsieur Bourgeois licen..."*

Suddenly, there was a guy behind me pushing me out of the office. "Hey...what the hell are you doing?" I shouted.

The angry guy said something to me in French. When I turned around to confront him, I made a fist and said a few things that John Wayne might say, his wife came into the office screaming, "*Gendarme! Gendarme!*" She was yelling for the police, and I was just an American in search of a tank of gasoline. Thinking of one of my friends back in Landstuhl who was grilled on and off for three years by the French police for having an automobile accident with a Frenchman, I refrained from hitting the rotund fellow. Instead, I made a gesture known throughout

123

the world but seldom used in international diplomacy. By this time, we were outside the station where my wife and kids could see everything that was happening. He made the same gesture, but the one the French used. I held my right hand to my head and made the sign for, "you're crazy." The fat guy made another non-verbal message by putting his hand in front of his nose and waving four of his fingers. Indeed, we were in a verbal cul-de-sac. By this time, my wife was in hysterics and could hardly get the words out of her lovely mouth.

"Get in the car, Harv," Chieko laughed.

"It's obvious that we aren't going to get any gas here, so I guess we'd better get the hell out of here before the police come," I said.

When we got to the next town, I stopped a police officer, and with the help of a young woman who volunteered to interpret, I told him what happened at the gas station. After listening to my story, he responded, "I recommend that you gas up only in the larger towns. You see, most of the small towns are communists."

I thanked both of them, then I climbed back into our car and continued driving onto the grand city of Paris.

Paris was a beautiful city filled with many things to do, and wonderful places to visit. We went to the Louvre where we saw scores of paintings and sculptures including the Venus de Milo statue, and the Mona Lisa. We walked over the many bridges that spanned the Seine River and visited the Eiffel Tower, and the Basilica of Sacre-Coeur in Montmartre. The Notre Dame Cathedral was both gargantuan and grandeur, and the steps of the church a fellow tried to sell me some porn pictures, however, I passed on his kind offer. On our final day in Paris, Chieko tried out her French. After looking at some items in a boutique shop, she replied to the woman working behind the counter, *"Merci boo boo."* We got a big laugh at the expense of Chieko's interpretation of the French language.

That wasn't my first trip to Paris. A year earlier, Chuck Jacobs and I took a two day trip to the City of Lights. After choosing a small hotel on the left bank, that could be best described as a house of ill repute, we headed out to see the town. The two of us visited the Eiffel Tower, the Louve, and the famous underground tombs. During our tour of the tombs, we noticed four young women staring at me and whispering among themselves. Although I hadn't planned on looking French, I was wearing a beret, and I had a mustache that made me look like a typical *Parisien.*

"Chuck, those American girls are giving us the once over. I think it would nice to go over and say hello to them. But, I've got an idea. I'm going to pretend to be a Frenchman. So just play along with me," I said.

"Sounds good to me," Chuck replied.

"Je m'appelle, Jacque Strappe," I proclaimed in my ersatz French accent.

"It's nice to meet you," the girls chorused. Then the girls introduced themselves.

Using my high school French, I replied in my phony French accent, *"Enchante."*

The young women explained that they had just graduated from nursing school and were touring Paris together.

"C'est tres bien," I replied. Then I asked them, "Would you be so kind to let me translate for you?"

"Oh, that would be wonderful!" They cried.

As the French tour guide explained the stories of each of the long deceased souls, I pretended to listen intently, and then I weaved intricate tales about the departed who lived a long time ago. I described how they each died tragic deaths that somehow involved love affairs. After the eighth tragic love story, I couldn't stand it anymore and broke out laughing.

"What so funny?" One of the girls asked.

I confessed to the hoax, and after their initial shock, they were really good sports. When the nurses stopped laughing, they asked us if they could stay with Chuck and I while we toured Paris. Of course we agreed, and the six of us toured the Arch de Triomphe, the Eiffel Tower, and for a walk along the Seine River. Before departing that evening, we got a final laugh at my French accent when I said,

"Bonne nuit et au revoir."

Farewell To Germany

The possibility that I might strangle my principal, and the dire financial situation made it nearly impossible to stay in Germany, so it was time for us to give up teaching with the Overseas Schools and return to the states. After submitting my resignation, I drove to the northern German town of Bremerhaven to ship my Volkswagen 1200 back to the states. On my return trip, I booked a space in a sleeping car on the train where I passed the long ride back to Landstuhl playing chess with a couple of German soldiers.

After getting back to Landstuhl, we packed our possessions and said our farewells to everyone. On the final night in the German town, we stayed in a hotel next to the railroad tracks. The train station was a fitting spot for the hotel because it was the kind of place where you had to bring your own light bulbs. And to make matters worse, we found out the next day that it was a whorehouse.

The United States

While preparing for our return to the United States, I had researched the base library and established a list of positive attributes that compared cities where we night live. After looking at several places, I came up with Seattle, Washington. The city had a couple of Buddhist temples, plenty of parks, and in spite of the excessive amount of rainfall, it enjoyed a fairly good climate.

Landing at Kennedy Airport, we took a taxi over to Bayonne, New Jersey to get our Volkswagen. From there, we started our long drive out to the West Coast. Passing through New Jersey, Pennsylvania, Ohio, and Illinois, we compared the differences in scenery in each of the states, while most of time, Yukihiro, Mitchell, and Michelle slept peacefully in the back seat. It was five o'clock in the morning, and on the outskirts of Chicago, we stopped to get a bag full of White Castle burgers for breakfast. Even at that early hour, the burgers tasted delicious.

Everything was going well until we reached Wisconsin. While driving through "America's Dairyland," we developed some engine trouble. Left with no choice, we pulled into a service station to get our Volkswagon repaired. As they were working on my German car, we overheard everything the two men said. I didn't know their real names, so for the sake of identification, I called them "Greasy" and "Oily."

"You know, Greasy, I had a girlfriend that looked just like her when I was stationed in Japan," the fellow named Oily bragged to his buddy.

"Really? Man! She's sure good looking. I'll betcha' you had some good times with her," Greasy said.

"I sure did. Yep. I sure did." Oily replied.

As they were wiping the grime off their hands, I asked, "Are you fellows almost finished?

Looking surprised, Greasy said, "Yep, we are done. You can go over to the office and pay your bill. But I gotta' tell you that you speak English real good."

"Thank you very much," I replied.

The next day, we were in Rapid City visiting with Connie Higa, and her son, Mark. Seeing her after three years was wonderful, and we had a great time during our stay at her home. Charlie was serving his second tour in Viet Nam, so he was gone for a year. All of us were worried about Higa-san, but each of us kept our thoughts to ourselves. After spending three days visiting the Black Hills National Park, and a few other places around Rapid City, we said our goodbyes and continued on our journey to Seattle.

Driving around the steep hills of Seattle was anything but pleasant. Urban renewal was a few years away, and to say the least, the scenery around the town was rather grim. Many of the buildings either needed to be painted, repaired, or torn down, and to top things off, it looked like it was going to rain at any moment. But we all agreed that we were hungry, so we parked our car on one of the town's many hills and found a nearby Chinese restaurant. As we entered the pedestrian looking establishment, we were underwhelmed by its lack of decor. We sat down at one of the tables and looked at the plastic covered menu. After examining the list, we decided on chop suey. Once the Chinese waiter delivered the meal to our table, all of us stared at the food for a minute before deciding that it was unfit for human consumption. First, we tried the rice, but it was old and lousy; it tasted like it had been the left in the rice pot for a couple of days. The chop suey was equally disgusting. After running our chopsticks through the food a couple of times, I said, "You know, this food is really awful. I don't think that I want to live in any town that serves this sort of swill!"

"I'm afraid that I have to agree," Chieko said.

"I say that we get out of here and head on down to San Francisco. Things have got to be better there. Any place worthy of being called a restaurant in San Francisco is a heck of lot better than this joint," I said.

San Francisco

Driving through the night, we arrived in San Francisco the next morning. Although it was during the Haight-Asbury era, and there were hippies everywhere, it was still a beautiful and captivating city to behold. It was summer time, but the weather was cool, and in contrast to Seattle, the sunshine had chased away the fog for a few hours. While walking the streets of the town looking for a place to live, we spotted a FOR RENT sign on a small building on Church Street.

We knocked on the front door and a middle-aged woman answered. "Yes, may I help you?"

Standing at the door was a grey haired woman wearing a dress with floral imprints, sensible shoes, and a smile on her round face.

"I see that you have a FOR RENT sign in the front of the apartment building. Would you mind showing us the apartment?" I asked.

"I'd be happy too," the rotund woman answered. "You know, this town is full of hippies who leave a mess and sleep on the floor. It would be wonderful to have a good family living here," the woman said. Her wide smile revealed a gold front tooth.

We ended up renting the two bedroom, one bath, unfurnished apartment, and quickly came to terms on how we were going to pay for it. That night, Yukihiro slept in the bedroom closet, while the rest of us slept on the floor like a bunch of hippies.

Cathy and Marvin Dwyer, who were friends of ours from Germany, moved to San Francisco the year before and settled into a very pleasant apartment on the Avenues. After we telephoned them, they asked us over to their place for lunch the next day. While eating bratwurst, we chatted about our times in Germany and the people that we knew. As we were leaving their place, Cathy offered some pots and pans to hold us over until our household goods arrived from overseas. A couple of days later, I bought a used television set for $25.00, and along with Cathy's pots and pans, we settled into our new apartment. My next task was to find a job.

At first, I tried the business world, but I was either overqualified or simply didn't have the experience for the positions. After ten days of searching the job market, I gave up on the business world and went to the Stanford University placement office to inquire about teaching jobs in the bay area. The following day, I received two interview offers. The first one went well, and I received an offer from the Freemont school district, but I ended up taking the job in Vallejo because I liked the fellow who interviewed me, Mike Cook. The assistant superintendent gave me a whirlwind tour of the town, as well as several of their schools. Afterwards, he joked that the trip was known as, "Cook's Tours."

Vallejo, California

We remained in San Franciso for a month before moving out to Vallejo. Our modern subsidized apartment had three bedrooms, two baths, a living and dining room, and lots of space for the kids to play. The four of us settled into the place and waited for our household goods to arrive from Germany.

I was teaching at Beverly Hills Elementary School, but don't let the name fool you. The school was in the poorest part of town and it was nothing like the Beverly Hills in Los Angeles. Chicanos and Blacks made up the majority of the population, but the kids were eager to learn, and that made the job much easier than it might have been. The lone exception was Cheryl Jones, who was as tough as nails, and could beat up every boy, girl, or teacher in the school. My friend, Bob Hunt, suffered through her hostility throughout the fifth grade, so the following year I volunteered to take her into my class. Learning that Cheryl attended Black Panther meetings every Tuesday night in Oakland, she was angry as hell at white folks on Wednesdays. Realizing the reasons behind her anger, I decided that I wouldn't resist her moods, but instead, embrace them. Every Tuesday after school, I would teach her Wednesdays math lessons so that she would be prepared to teach them the next day. The following day, she would instruct the lessons to the students, and I can tell you that not creature stirred, not even a mouse while Cheryl was teaching the class. I had discovered a way to temper her anger, while at the same time, capitalize on her need to be a leader. The result was that the kids, and Cheryl, learned a hell of lot of mathematics that year.

At the end of the school year she commented, "Mr. Getz, we had some rough times, but I really learned a lot this year."

I felt good about the comment, even when later that summer, I read in the newspaper that Cheryl Jones stabbed a girl to death.

Maria lived in our same apartment complex in Vallejo when she met Bob Hunt. At first, things were somewhat uneasy for the troubled couple. Simply put, she wanted to marry him, but he wasn't cooperating. So there were many nights when we tried to convince Maria not to give up the thought of marrying Bob. By remaining, patient, everything eventually worked out for the couple. Several months later, Bob Hunt and Maria Estrella were married in front of family and friends in Mexico City.

Our third son, Daniel, was born about a year after we moved to Vallejo. About to leave the comfort of the womb, I called the hospital to tell them we were on our way. The nurse told me to chill out and give my wife an aspirin to relax her and not to bother coming to the hospital. As far as she was concerned, it was a false alarm. But she didn't know my wife, when Chieko said it was time for her to deliver the baby, you can be sure that it was time for the baby to wiggle out of her womb. In my own sweet way, I told the nurse what she could do with her aspirin, and that we were coming to the hospital.

Just minutes after arriving at the hospital, Chieko delivered our baby. He was healthy as a horse, and we named him Daniel.

During my third year at the school, the same year that Tug McGraw, who later became a star pitcher with the New York Mets and fathered country singer, Tim McGraw, was a substitute teacher at Beverly Hills School. I remember him well because he always wore the same brown suit and showed films of his baseball training camps to his kids. At the beginning of the year, I was asked by our principal, Mr. Harry Thorn, to become the school's Home-Community Advisor. Helping parents of the children who were either in trouble, or didn't come to school was my main responsibility. I became accustomed to seeing laundry on couches and houses that were sometimes a bit messy inside, but most of the people were very kind. It was an interesting and satisfying job that required people skills and a willingness to listen to the various problems that confronted both parents and kids. A professor from San Francisco State College came out to the school every week to observe my program, and he must have liked what he saw because he offered me a fellowship in special education and a six thousand dollar a year stipend. I was about to accept the position when I learned of a fellowship at San Jose State that offered a masters degree and a lifetime credential in guidance and counseling. It also paid a stipend of nine thousand dollars for the year including tuition costs. Not letting the opportunity pass me by, I drove to San Jose and interviewed with Professor Braxton, the head honcho of the program. I told Dr. Braxton everything what he wanted to hear from a fellow liberal, and two weeks later, I received a fellowship in guidance and counseling from San Jose State University.

San Jose State University

Carmen Rodriquez, Calvin Michaels, Helen O'Donald, John Jackson (a former wide receiver for the St. Louis Cardinals), and Sid Stewart were just a few of the twenty graduate students accepted into the program. We all became good friends and hung out together both in and out of school. It was during my first semester at San Jose State, that I learned the professor who worked with me in Vallejo had committed suicide. Somehow, I felt that if I had gone to San Francisco State, I might have made a difference.

The super bowl was on television, and we were invited to Sid Stewart's apartment for an afternoon of football and something good to eat. That something was Sid's chilli that he had spent several hours behind the hot stove cooking up. As for the football game, Joe Kapp, Minnesota's quarterback, was dominated by Len Dawson, Kansas City's thrower by a score of 23-10 at New Orlean's Tulane Stadium. On the other hand, Chieko and I were defeated by Sid's chilli. Seldom had we tasted something that good, but so spicy and full of fart inducing ingredients that we immediately started passing gas. As a matter of fact, for the next week, both of us experienced sudden attacks that would send any dog or cat running for their four-legged lives. The chilli was really good going down, but it was the coming back up that was the problem. Anyway, to this day, we are still friends with the deadly chilli making Sid Stewart and his wife, Vicki.

During breaks in our busy day, we would often gather at the student union to discuss politics with Harry Edwins, a civil rights leader, sports representative, and professor. Also at the bull sessions was Jim Karlos, a gold medal winner, and one of the runners who gave the black power salute at the 1968 Olympics. Because the group had several Chicanos/Chicanas who were active in the Cesar Chavez movement, we were being closely watched by at least one far-right group. Some of the Mexican-Americans reported that their cars and homes were bombarded with feces and other unpleasantries. As for me, my phone was tapped so I had to be very careful what I said over the phone.

My fieldwork included eight weeks at an elementary school, and another eight weeks at Pioneer High School. My two months at the elementary level consisted of mainly being mostly ignored, and during my eight weeks at the high school, I was completely overlooked. One incident that occurred at the elementary school was when a little third grader forgot his lunch money, and that meant no food for the little guy. Keeping in mind that his mother may not have had the money to buy his lunch that day, the lad may not forgotten his lunch money at all. He just didn't have the money. A female teacher, a Japanese-American who endured the hardships of living in an American concentration camp, really laid into him as he stood in the middle of the cafeteria crying. Before she was finished reaming him out, I walked over to the boy and handed him some money for his lunch. After the teacher was finished with the lad, he turned to me and thanked me, then ran over to the lunch line to get his food.

A month later, I reported to Pioneer High School to complete the high school segment of my internship. One of the school's guidance counselors greeted me with a few unfriendly words before tellng me to go over to the metal building that stood at the far end of the campus. "That's where the Mexican-American kids are housed. You can work with them in there." With those final words our conversation came to a close, and he turned and left me standing alone in the parking lot.

I entered the portable building curious as to what kind of reception I would receive. Would they accept me, or would they be hostile and mistrusting? Perhaps they might simply ignore me. True to the guidance counselor's words, sitting around shooting the breeze was a group of Mexican-American kids. The leader of the group was a lad named Luis Gomez who, after speaking with me for a few moments, introduced me to the students before showing me to my desk. It took a few days for the students to warm up to me, but as time went by, they became increasingly friendly. Since I was going to be there for eight weeks, I thought that I might as well try to teach them some mathematics, social studies, and English. In turn, they taught me Chicano history. After a week or so passed, and as an act of acceptance into their group, they invited me to have lunch at one of their favorite eateries. Half of the group got into my large Ford LTD, and the other half of the class jumped into a student's car. Since they could do anything they wanted at Pioneer High School, except go to class, they often went out to lunch. As we sped down the highway, we managed to get a few stares from the other cars. Although a few years earlier my car had been one of Ford's top models, but now, it blew out a lot of oil making it an environmental hazard. Californians were beginning to think about the pollution of their air, so that wasn't a good thing. But we gave a hearty laugh while continuing down the road to our small but excellent Mexican restaurant.

Luis Gomez was a handsome guy who fancied himself a Chicano labor movement historian. He knew all the names and dates that were important to the La Raza movement, and could recite the major points of Cesar Chavez's speeches. This kid had talent and charisma, but he was trapped between his immense pride and the prejudice he faced. After a month of watching Luis lead his fellow students in discussions, I went to the La Raza office on the San Jose State campus to share with them Luis' many talents. The people at the office asked me to bring him over to the university so they could talk with the young man. Impressed by his intelligence and leadership ability, after interviewing Luis, they offered him a full scholarship, but with the condition that he graduate from high school. This meant genuflecting to the white administrators and teachers at Pioneer High School, this was something that Luis couldn't do.

My year at San Jose State was in its final quarter when I walked over to the placement office to see what jobs might be available to me after I graduated. One announcement posted on the wall caught my eye. It was a job advertising a counseling position at the Singapore American School. Reading over the offer, I decided that I was very interested in the job, so I took down the letter and stuffed it in my pocket.

When I got home, I showed the announcement to Chieko.

"Yes, of course," she replied, "I'd love to go to Singapore. It would be a very exciting experience for us. C'mon, let's try for it."

Later that evening, I sat down and wrote a letter to Dr. Edward McNair, superintendent of the Singapore American School, explaining that I would soon be graduating with a masters degree in guidance and counseling and that I was very interested in the position. A few weeks later, I was prepared to show up at the St. Francis Hotel in San Francisco for an interview, but there was a crises involving my students at Pioneer High School, and instead, I attended the meeting rather than going to San Francisco for my interview. But ten days later, I received a phone call from Dr. McNair, who happened to be in San Jose for the day. He asked me whether I was still interested in the position. I answered that I was still interested in the job, but that I hadn't attended the interview because there was a problem at my school that day. After agreeing to come to his motel room, he requested that I bring my wife to the interview. Now somewhat concerned about Chieko, because if the fellow was a bloody racist I wanted no part of the job and I would tell him so before leaving the meeting. We drove to the motel and I knocked on the door. We waited patiently for him to answer, but instead, a beautiful Asian woman came to the door and invited us in to the room where Dr. McNair greeted us. A few minutes later, we learned that the woman was his new wife and that she was Indonesian. That answered my concerns about his feelings on race and international marriages.

The four of us sat on his bed and finally came to terms with my salary. During the negotiations, I promised to find another guidance counselor for the high school position. That person was Helen O'Donald, a woman in our graduate group. Sid Stewart, the fart-inducing chili maker and close friend, was appointed to the counseling position at nearby Kuala Lumpur, Malaysia.

Chieko and the kids left San Jose a month early so that the three of them could spend time on Okinawa visiting with her parents and friends. Now alone, I moved into a house with fellow graduate student, Calvin Michaels and his good-looking girlfriend. Calvin was a black guy with a penchant for pretty women, motorcycles, and athletics. He originally left Harlem to high dive competitively, but he also had to get out of New York in order to save his own life. It seems there were some gang members back in the "Big Apple" who wanted him dead. However, he was now safely tucked away at San Jose State University surrounded by friends and having the time of his life.

Since I had a job waiting for me in Singapore, I received permission from the San Jose authorities to take my test a week earlier than the other students. For the entire six hours of the exam, I wrote about what I read during the past ten months and answered all the questions on the test. After I finished the exam, I was pretty confident that I had passed it.

The day following my comprehensives, Calvin drove me to the San Francisco airport where we talked over lunch before bidding each other a fond farewell.

Tokyo

After a thirteen-hour flight from San Francisco, we made a smooth landing at Tokyo's International Airport. As I made my way to the front of the plane, I noticed that a young woman was having problems as she maneuvered through the dark aisle with her baby and her suitcase. At that moment, I thought about my wife and how I would want someone to help her if she were in the same situation, so I squeezed my way up the aisle and asked, "May I help you to get off the plane?"

"Yes, that would be very nice. Thank you very much," the woman smiled. Even in the dark, I could see that she was Asian and good looking.

"I'll tell what. You take the baby and I'll carry the bag," I said.

A few minutes later, we found two seats together then we waited for the bus driver to fill out a couple of forms before driving us into Tokyo. While riding to the hotel, we shared a few things about ourselves. She was going to Korea to visit her husband, who was in the US Army, as well as spend some time with her family and friends. I explained that I was on my way to Okinawa to join my wife and children, then it was off to Singapore to be a guidance counselor at the Singapore American School. When we arrived at the hotel, located on the Ginza, I offered to carry her son while she carried the bag. While waiting in the hotel lobby for our rooms, although I didn't know what he was doing at the time, the Japanese fellow in charge of room assignments took us to the same room. Apparently the man thought we were married. And we were, but not to each other. Although the arrangement may or may not have been fine with the young woman, I called the desk and asked for my own room.

After taking off my clothes to take a bath, the Korean woman called and asked if I wanted to go out and tour the Ginza. "All right," I said, "but I have to take a bath first. I'll call you back later."

I soaked in the warm water for about thirty minutes, then climbed out of the bathtub, dried off, and stretched out on the bed for a few moments. The next thing I heard was the sound of my telephone.

"Good morning. I guess we missed each other last night," said the Korean woman. "How about meeting me for breakfast?"

"Wow! I was relaxing for just a few moments and I guess I was out like a light."

"That's all right. Let's meet downstairs and have breakfast before you go onto Okinawa," she said.

"Sounds good to me," I replied, "I'll meet you downstairs in fifteen minutes."

No sooner had I hung up the phone when it rang again. It was one of the hotel employees. "Mr. Getz, you must come right away. Your taxi is waiting to take you to the airport."

After hanging up the phone, I searched for the paper with the woman's room number on it, but I couldn't find it and I didn't have time to look for the darn thing. Left with no other choice, I quickly dressed and rushed down the stairs and out to my taxi.

Waiting in the taxi was another passenger, but this time she was Japanese. The young woman spoke English quite well, which made it easy to carry on a conversation with the good-looking woman traveling to Italy to continue with her budding operatic career. A half an hour later, after talking about a variety of things, we arrived at Tokyo International Airport and said our goodbyes.

Okinawa

The Island of Smiles hadn't changed much over the past eight years. Most people welcomed Americans everywhere, and the shops and markets flourished with goods from Japan and America. Highway One was still lined with military surplus shops, car lots, and restaurants.

After arriving in Nakadomari, I gathered up my family and moved into the nearby Yamada Onsen Hotel; a small hotel where we slept on the tatami mats. Every evening, Mitchell and I went for a refreshing swim in the East China Sea to soak in the warm water and take in the beauty of the sea. Because the small hotel was an *Onsen*, it had natural sulfur baths, so we all scrubbed and soaked ourselves at the bath house a couple times each day.

Daniel and Yumiko had a good time visiting with their grandparents and going to the playground on top of the Yamagataya Department Store in Naha. Little Daniel turned out to be quite a dancer. Whenever he heard Okinawan music played on the radio, he would dance with the same intricate hand motions as used by the locals. Dancing on his grandparent's table, we wondered where Daniel had learned to dance like a Ryukyuan native.

After spending a week on the island, it was time for us to continue on to Singapore. We said *sayonara* to everyone, then continued on to another great adventure.

Singapore

Following a short stopover in Hong Kong, we arrived in Singapore where Dr. McNair, our school superintendent, was at Changi Airport to greet us. After the usual salutations, we climbed into Dr. McNair's car, and his driver took us to our new home on Jalan Mera Saga.

Before we had the chance to put our suitcases down, we saw that our dinner table was full of food and drink, and a maid was standing by to attend to our every need. The house was typical of those in the better parts of Singapore. It had four bedrooms and a bath upstairs, a large living and dining room, a fully equipped kitchen, and a maid's quarters complete with its own bathroom and kitchen. Outside the house, there was a small playground in the backyard. The floors of the house were made of marble so that it was easy for the maid to wash. The only disadvantage was that the house was located just across from the British army flats. This meant that, occasionally, we had to shoo away some British boys who invaded our kitchen looking for something good to eat. However, they weren't the only pests who came into the house without an invitation. Because the house was open in the back, armies of ants would march into our living room. Without a trace of mercy or compassion, we poured boiling water on the insects to get rid of the little buggers. One afternoon, a funny thing happened when Daniel was about to get an outdoor bath that our maid had prepared for him. Daniel got into the water then he screamed, "I'm no ant. I'm no ant. It's too hot!"

While Michelle and Daniel were both too young to attend school, Yukihiro, Mitchell, and I, following breakfast, would make our way to the Singapore American School. Sometimes, we rode the Ford Counsel that I parked facing downward on the hill in front of our house. After a little push, it usually would start, but sometimes, the car refused to respond to my Herculean efforts. When the car refused to turn over, we would either take a cab or walk to school. After school was over for the day, we walked through what remained of a jungle village and came out the other side of the bushes to the twentieth century. In the village, everyone seemed to have a purpose in life. The old people took care of the little ones, the women cooked and cleaned, and the men went out to work in the fields. Because it was one of the last jungle villages, or *kampongs* in Singapore, it was a very pleasant but ephemeral setting. However, the native people were powerless to do anything about the various changes taking place in their once orderly society. Most of the villagers were forced into what were called, "New Towns." These were a collection of multi-family apartments with shops and restaurants located on the first floor of the buildings. Many of those former *Kampong* residents leaped out the windows of their crowded dwellings to their deaths because they no longer had a purpose in the new society. The Singapore government didn't publish reports on the number of people who committed suicide because the bureaucrats figured that it was one of the minor kinks in the wheel that was driving Singapore toward the future.

At the Singapore American School, my responsibilities included counseling elementary students, as well as administering entrance tests to students from around the world. After examining the results of the examination, I would place them into their appropriate grade levels. Helping me to carry out my duties were two female secretaries. One was a Sephardic Jew, and the other woman was Chinese. Both were competent, efficient, and lovely. Because the school had two sessions, I was finished by twelve-thirty and I was free to go home to enjoy the rest of the day. There were times when I went downtown for a drink and traveled around the city, but most of the time, I played badminton or basketball with the teachers in the school's gym.

A fifth grade female teacher tried, but failed to harness an Israeli boy who violated almost every rule we had at the school. His parents would come to the school to plead the case that he should remain a student at Singapore American School. His father was the Israeli ambassador, and his wife, a worried Jewish mother who just wanted her son to adjust to the demands that the school required. The third time they came to school, the ambassador pulled the "we are fellow Jews" card. That was when I took a different approach. I took the boy out of the woman teacher's class and placed him with Mr. Coleman, an Englishman. He was a fair man, but he didn't take any crap from anyone, including the Israeli ambassador's son. Coleman was a fellow who drove around in a MG sports car with a monkey on his shoulder and competed in Malaysian car rallies. Occasionally, I would ride downtown with him, and he would scare the living daylights out of me. But he was a good driver, even with his last second stops at the red lights and stop signs. Coleman's monkey was also a bit of a daredevil, too. Unfortunately, the poor animal met up with a terrible accident when he fell out of a tree and broke his arm.

I took the Israeli boy over to Mr. Coleman and explained the circumstances to him.

"Sure. I'll take him. But I have to say something to him first," Mr. Coleman said.

"Please say to him whatever you want. This is his last chance to stay at our school," I replied

Coleman grabbed the lad and put him up against the wall. Then the Englishman warned him, "If I ever hear a peep out of you, then you are going to be bloody sorry. Do we understand each other?"

"Yes...yes...sir," replied the lad.

The boy from Israel had met his match, and he never had another incident while at the Singapore American School.

At a local basketball tournament, our faculty team played a Chinese High School teachers team and lost badly. But it wasn't because we weren't any good. We weren't star-studded, but our squad had a couple of former college players, so we probably were better than the team that beat us. But the Chinese referees and the audience simply wouldn't allow an American team to win, no matter how good we were. Although our guys weren't even close to the players they allegedly fouled, within fifteen minutes, the best players on our team had fouled out of the game. Now, with only two players remaining, I entered the game. After receiving the ball from one of my teammates, I dribbled halfway up the court only to be covered by two of their players. I stopped dribbling, but I had no one to pass the ball to because the other two guys were also covered. Left with nothing else to do, I faked to my left, and then to my right, then I shot the ball. Miraculously, from half court, I swished the ball smack into the center of the basket for two points. The other team figured that I was the ringer, and from that moment on. I was constantly covered by two guys, and I didn't get off another shot.

Bob Magnussen, a former UCLA basketball player who played third string on Kareem Abdul Jabbar's team, announced to our faculty basketball team that Dave Brubeck was coming to town for a concert, and it would be a great idea if we took our wives to the see the show

Unfortunately, a couple of reprehensible government officials got in the way of the ill-fated concert. When Brubeck and his quartet arrived at Changi Airport, they were told that it was impossible for them to enter Singapore with long hair. The government employees offered to give the guys haircuts, but Dave Brubeck turned down their generous offer.

Well, so much for the Dave Brubeck concert. Later in the year, Nancy Wilson came to town and we went to see her perform. She was marvelous, and so was her trio of shorthaired musicians.

A old friend from the past unexpectedly showed up in Singapore while I was in the upstairs hallway of the cold storage (supermarket). I was shooting a film about Orchard Road, when a young woman carrying a little girl, and walking with another young girl, sauntered passed me in the deserted second-story hallway. After the pretty, but strangely familiar woman walked by me, I realized who she was. Surprised as hell, I shouted, "BARBARA MONROE!" After hearing her name, she turned around to face me. It was the girl that I once admired in her green plaid bathing suit at Altoona's Lakemont Park. Although I was shocked to see her in Singapore, she wasn't all that surprised to see me. During our conversation, she said that she had somewhat of an advantage over me because she knew that I was working at the school. Now living in Singapore, her husband, Dave Roberts, the Penn State electrical engineer, and the fellow that she ditched me for, was managing a local electronics factory.

We talked for a few minutes, but when I asked her if she wanted to sit down somewhere, she quickly ended our conversation and departed in a bit of a huff. The truth was that her daughter, who she was holding, seemed a bit heavy for Barbara and that is why I asked her if she wanted to find place to sit down. But a few weeks later, she called me to invite us to her home for dinner. A week after that, Chieko invited them to our house and we continued to enjoy the company of Barbara and Stan Roberts until we left Singapore five months later.

Because the school board was conservative, while most of the American teachers were liberals, the two opposing philosophies didn't mix well. At the end of the school year, after a great deal of controversy with the superintendent, most of the teachers from California and New York gave up their positions and returned to the United States. I was one of those educators.

On our way back to California, we stopped in Okinawa for a brief vacation before returning to the states. Once again, we stayed at the Yamada Onsen where we enjoyed swimming in the East China Sea and taking hot sulfur baths at the hotel. While there, Yukihiro decided to remain with his grandparents and look for a job. The Viet Nam war was going strong, so we supported his decision to remain on Okinawa. Yukihiro got a position with Trans-World Airways and remained on the island until they shut down their operations sometime during the late seventies. A short time later, Yuki moved to Hawaii to take a job with a tourist company, and he later married his Okinawan sweetheart, Michiko-san.

Napa, California

After returning to California, we stayed in a small apartment in Vallejo while we looked for a permanent place to live. One house in Vallejo that we looked at had some pretty obnoxious neighbors. While walking in the backyard of the house, standing on the other side of the fence were several people with arms folded and angry looks on their pasty faces. Apparently they didn't want us there, which meant that we didn't want to be there either. Quickly passing on the house, we went out to Napa where they were building some new homes on Tokay Drive. Once we saw the model home, we bought it and waited for the workers to finish building the house.

Moving to Napa was a good decision. The scenery was beautiful with its vineyards, wineries, rolling hills, and clean air. Now that we were settled into our new home, I was kept busy building fences, a deck, and landscaping the place.

Franklin Junior High School

During my nine years as a guidance counselor at Franklin Junior High School, even with great colleagues like Leticia Drake, Rich Charles, Jamie Goldberg, and Alphonzo Bellomo, I did little to make a mark on the school. On the other hand, my colleagues made a positive impression on me. One summer vacation, Leticia Drake returned to her roots in Sicily, and while riding down *La via Etnea* in Catania admiring the scenes of her beloved homeland, a thief reached inside the taxi and stole her purse. Alphonzo Bellomo, another Sicilian-American, was a gentle and loving man who remained calm even in moments of adversity. The extremely competent counselor was one of the world's nicest people, and he was a true friend who always came to work with a smile on his wonderful Sicilian face.

Occasionally, I'd go skiing with Jamie Goldberg and her then boyfriend, physical education teacher, Angel Ramos. After a day on the slopes, while traveling back to Napa, we stopped in Placerville to get something to eat. While walking to a restaurant, we saw a man lying on the sidewalk; my friends thought that he was just a bum having a pleasant rest. But I didn't. I stopped to help the man sit up, and that is when he told me that he had just had a heart attack and he needed a doctor. While I stayed with the fellow, Angel called for an ambulance to take him to the hospital. When Jamie asked me what made me stop to help the man, I replied, "It was his shoes. You see, they were polished, and that is why I knew that he wasn't a bum."

Franklin Junior High School could be a fairly rough place at times, but the counseling end of it wasn't bad. As the years went by, it became fairly predictable and even a bit boring. There were times, however, when the unexpected happened. It was the lunch hour, and while I was walking across the blacktop courtyard to the cafeteria some guy snuck up from behind and grabbed me around my neck. A few years had gone by since I practiced judo, but nevertheless the lad attacked me from behind, so it was an easy throw. Over my shoulder and on to the ground he went in one quick move. The kid was over six feet tall, and his friends who were watching from the side of the courtyard were amazed by my throw. As for me, I acted as if nothing happened and kept on walking to the cafeteria. A couple of days later, the guy was sent back to juvenile hall after assaulting a girl in the corridor of our school.

While watching the students pass through the hallway, a youngster came up to me and told me that some guy had a gun hidden in his pocket. I asked him to point out the student and tell me where the gun was located. The boy pointed to a fellow wearing a blue plaid shirt, and he answered, "in the left pocket." I strolled over to the left side of the hallway, and as he walked by, I grabbed the gun. I didn't know what kind it was, but it was big pistol of some sort. The police were called, and they hauled him off to the police station.

Our head secretary, Margaret Midler, ran the school, and no teacher or administrator ever dared to defy her. At the end of each exhausting day, we sat on the main office bench quietly waiting for the clock to turn to three o'clock, the official end of our work day. Finally, the hand turned, and as if a starting gun had gone off, everybody got up and said our goodbyes for the day. By the next morning, we were refreshed and ready for another round of educating our reluctant students.

My Running Career

I began working on my doctorate degree in administration at Nova Southeastern University in 1977, and after three years of classes, and another year working on my project, I was awarded the degree in 1981. During that time, our kids were growing like a field of corn. Mitchell was in high school, Michelle was in junior high school, and Dan was in elementary school. Chieko worked at a leather coat-making company before she opened her own store, *The Japanese Gourmet.* Managing the store and teaching cooking lessons kept her very busy, but in 1981, after two years of selling Japanese goods, we closed up the place for the simple reason that the only people making any money was the Japan Food Corporation.

In the fall of 1979, I began my running career at the American Canyon five-kilometer race, a residential area located midway between Vallejo and Napa. It was at that race that I learned there was a big difference between jogging and racing--it was speed. I began to seriously train, and it wasn't long before I was running sixty-five miles or more a week. On Thursday evenings, a group of runners would meet at Lou Dawson's house and run eight miles as fast as our skinny legs would carry us. Afterwards, we headed to a local restaurant for some beer, laughs, and pizza. On Saturdays and Sundays we ran our ten-kilometer races around Napa, Sonoma, and Solano counties.

My pal, Lou Dawson, called me one Saturday morning to run a marathon on the following day. I thought he was crazy, but I agreed, and I guess this made me kind of nuts, too. So the next morning, the two of us snuck off the Sacramento to run the forty-two kilometer marathon. I ended up running the race in three hours and twenty-nine minutes. A fairly decent pace considering that I hadn't prepared for it. At the end of the race, I wasn't tired, so I knew that I could have run it faster. My next marathon was in Oakland, and I finished the twenty-six mile race in three hours and nine minutes. The following spring, I ran three hours and two minutes in the San Francisco Marathon.

At the Lake Tahoe Relay, I set a course record on the final leg of the race. The first leg, Lou Dawson ran his usual outstanding race up the mountain. The second runner, Jim Heath was terrific. The third leg, run by Greg Hanson, was also great. However, the next round was our downfall. Mike Tsakiris was a runner who could run two marathons a week, but he was really slow that day, so we lost ten minutes against our chief rival, the Fairfield team. The next runner, Chuck Trudeau, ran well and made up for some of the time. When Mark Sullivan ran his leg of the race, he made a Herculean effort to make up even more of the time, but we were still four minutes behind. I was running the final leg of the race, and now it was my turn. My competition was a sub-three hour marathoner, which meant that I probably had little to no chance of catching him. On the other hand, being four minutes behind wasn't going to keep me from trying to win the race. Three miles into the run, I saw a blue speck a mile up the serpentine mountain road. It was only a dot at the time, but I knew that I just might catch the guy who was wearing a blue tee shirt. Finally, at mile seven, I caught up to him and passed the surprised but exhausted runner. When I got to the top of the next hill, one of his teammates, who was recording the times because they planned on setting a course record, was waiting for his teammate. But when he saw me instead, he was shocked and very pissed.

"Getz. What the F--k are you doing here. I'm gonna' break both your f--ken legs!"

It was high up in the mountains and the air was so thin that I couldn't get enough oxygen to breathe properly. But it didn't matter because I was going to win the race or die trying. As luck would have it, I didn't die, and by the end of the race, I beat the sub-three hour marathoner by four minutes. After the race was over, we celebrated our victory by downing a few beers with the team that we had defeated, the Fairfield boys.

During the weekdays, I would often run with a female runner, Bernice Silva. One of the runs was a killer course that began with a gigantic one-mile hill and then eased off for three miles before we ran back down the hill. But most of the time, I trained alone on my Dry Creek and Yountville course.

In 1981, growing bored with working at Franklin Junior High School, I began searching for new and interesting places to work. Going to Europe or Asia was what I had in mind, so I applied to the Department of Defense Schools. But there were no openings in guidance and counseling that year so I applied again in 1982. It was just after returning from a ten-kilometer race that I found a booklet on the table containing information on the Azores, Portugal. I thumbed through the book and wondered why the Department of Defense Schools sent it to me. A week later, after coming home from a Saturday half-marathon, I picked up the book and, once again, leaped through it, but this time, between pages thirty-two and thirty-three, I discovered a letter offering me a position in the Azores. The following Monday morning, I called Washington to find out if the job was still open. It was still available, and I eagerly accepted the offer.

The Azores

By the middle of August, I was off to the Azores to begin a new phase in my career as a guidance counselor. Teachers, as well as everyone else working for the U.S. government, weren't permitted to have their families with them until they secured a place to live. After spending the night in Philadelphia, I traveled on a C-141 to the Azores, Portugal. Upon my arrival at Lajes Field, my principal, Jack Richards, met me at the terminal and drove me to my BOQ. A few days later, I made friends with a couple of Americans who were contract civilian engineers temporarily assigned to the Azores. Besides touring the island together and going out to eat everyday, both fellows went with me on my house hunting expeditions. Word was out that a lieutenant commander, his wife, and their dog, had recently moved out of their house in Praia, so we went down to Cruz Street to look at the place. By American standards it wasn't very nice, but it was the best house we had seen so far.

After walking through the house, we exited out onto Cruz Street. "By the way, my principal lives right across the street," I said

"That's nice. Say, Harv, weren't you wearing white socks," noted one of my buddies.

I looked down at my athletic socks and they were now black as a panther. I yelled, "Jezus, those are fleas. There are fleas everywhere, dammit!"

My friends discovered that their socks were also covered with fleas. So there we were, three guys desperately brushing the damned things from our socks and pants in the middle of the cobblestone street. Finally rid of all the critters, we retreated back to the BOQ, and for the next two weeks, I ran through the flea-ridden house with a can of spray in each hand hoping that they would die an agonizing death. Finally, I removed the carpet that held the remainder of the fleas, and at last, they were gone.

Island bombs were the main form of transportation in the Azores. The humidity on the island was very high causing most automobiles to rust out quickly. I had a two door Buick with a vinyl top that was shredded in various places making the roof look as if it were coated with leaves. When my family arrived, I drove to the diminutive air terminal to pick them up in my island bomb. When Michelle saw the car, she stubbornly refused to get in the damned thing. But after a couple of minutes of persuasion, she finally climbed into the back seat and ducked down so that no one would see her. It wasn't long, however, before she learned that everyone had cars like mine in the Azores. In fact, ours was one of the better American cars on the island.

It was our first Christmas in the Azores and it was also winter break for the college students. Mitchell was coming for his first visit from the University of California at Santa Barbara, but to make a long story short, Mitchell didn't come and Chieko had a case of the blues. Michelle, Daniel, and I did our best to console her, but nothing seemed to work. Finally, I came up with an idea. It was time for a vacation and I had just the place--Madrid. At first, Chieko resisted, but Michelle and Daniel talked her into going on a space-available flight. It so happened that a National Guard flight from Ohio was stopping in the Azores to gas up, and then it was flying on to Madrid. This meant that if there was space on the plane, we would be going to Spain.

There was plenty of room on the C-130, and we were on our way to Madrid. Sitting in our bucket seats, the crew was very friendly, and the box lunches were fine with us. The only problem during the flight was when it was time to land, the pilot couldn't get the landing gear down. After trying a few of the standard ways to lower it, and failing, they resorted to removing one of the side panels and hand pumping the gears. It worked, and we made a safe landing at Torrejon Air Base.

After settling in at the Torrejon Inn, we caught a bus into Madrid and walked around the city revelling in many of the same things that the three million residents of the capital city enjoyed. Strolling around the central part of Madrid, we shopped in the department stores, had *paella* at one of the outdoor restaurants, toured the Prado museum, and roamed around the Plaza Major. The only negative thing about the trip to Spain was that Chieko had a couple of her skirts stolen while staying at the lodge.

The crew, who we ran into a few times on the streets of Madrid, managed to have engine problems, a common practice with National

Guard and Air Force reserve crews who traveled to such far away and exotic places as Madrid. They managed to stay grounded long enough for us to take the same plane back to Lajes Field.

After we were missing a shovel, we learned that you didn't leave anything outside unless you planned on getting rid of it. The Azoreans were a poor but honest people, and many of them lived in dirt floored houses with few of the conveniences that we enjoyed in most American homes. If we left a shovel or a rake outside for the night, it was gone by the next morning. The kindly Azorean people didn't regard that as stealing. Instead, they believed that if you left it outside, you didn't want it anymore.

Halloween was a time when both children and adults, without costumes, would swarm to the houses of the Americans for candy. Once we handed out all of our treats, we locked the doors, shut off the lights and pretended that we weren't home.

On my daily runs through the island's villages, I would see girls standing outside their houses eating elongated strips of oil with tiny bits of meat. Although we didn't touch that stuff, one of our favorite meals was Alcatra, a tender rump roast dish cooked for several hours and served with french fries and a glass of Portuguese red wine.

A couple of months later, we moved out of our place on Cruz Street to a base house located just across the road from the officers club. It was a duplex, and on the other side of us was the Valentine family. Ken Valentine, a science teacher, liked to play his stereo as loud as humanly possible without breaking the sound barrier. And the worst part of it was that it was organ music, the kind that sounded like a funeral was taking place in his house. Finally, I had enough of the racket and went next door to tell him to turn the bloody thing down. His little boy answered the door then screamed his fool head off at the sight of me. Ken came to the door as if nothing was wrong with having his son scream in my face.

"How you doing, Harv?"

"Not bad," I said. "Say Ken, I was wondering if you could turn that funeral music down a little bit?"

"Wow! I thought you liked it. That's why I have the speakers turned against wall. It's so you can hear it better."

"To be honest, Ken, I don't like it at all," I replied.

"Really. I thought you liked it." He seemed disappointed.

At that point, he walked over to where the speakers were located, then he turned them back around to face his living room instead of mine. That solved the problem of the loud funeral music. The sounds of Miles Davis, Stan Getz, Bill Evans, and Mel Torme, where, once again, the dominant sounds in our living room.

Ken swore that foam was a remedy for the cancerous rust that ate our cars. So every time there was a rust mark, he would fill it with the foamy stuff. One day, he was driving around the corner near our house when his Chevy convertible broke in half. His car had finally reached its limit of foam and the Chevy Corvair could take no more. Well, so much for foam as a body repair panacea. We got a big laugh out of his tragedy, and since he couldn't foam the two pieces of the island bomb back into one piece, Ken junked it.

Night fell on the Azores, and the only light in the evening sky came from the quarter moon that danced in and out of the clouds. Up in the tree, like a couple of unpicked apples, were two ninjas patiently waiting for their prey to appear. With *shuriken* at the ready, and *nunchucks* in hand, they were prepared to strike a blow for freedom loving peoples everywhere. Suddenly, from out of the darkness, a lone figure cut through the silent evening unaware of the danger that awaited him. As he approached the tree, two masked figures wearing ninja suits dropped to the ground and scared the loving shit out of the youngster. The boy saw the two ninjas snarling at him, but there was nothing he could do about it but run screaming and crying back to his house.

One of those ninjas was my son, Daniel. A few weeks later, his partner was caught on the roof of the headquarters building getting ready for his next victim. Fortunately, the boy's father was a colonel, so nothing really happened to him. But the threat of the ninjas in the Azores was over.

One thing that my daughter had no doubts about was the day after she graduated from Lajes High School, she was returning to Napa to resume the life that she had once known. I heard this several times during the first five months in the Azores, but one spring morning, while having breakfast, Michelle asked, "Dad, could I stay on Lajes when you guys go back to the states for the summer?"

The answer was an unequivocal "No!" But I nearly fell off of my chair when she asked me the question. Here was the young lady who was going to return to Napa as soon as she possibly could. But in the past six months, she had become a world traveler and was no longer interested in returning to California. *Why I'll be a monkey's uncle*, I said to myself.

I ran several races while on the island, but first place always went to Ju'an, who missed running in the Olympics by less than a second. I came in at the number two spot, and third place belonged to a twenty-two year old guy who ran in street shoes. Feeling secure with second place, I gave the guy a pair of my old running shoes, and from that time on, the kid managed to beat me by a second or two.

Approaching the village, on my final leg of a long run in the countryside, just outside the airport runway fence, a farmer shouted something at me. But the only Portuguese I knew was, *Noa Faz Mal* (It doesn't matter). I kept running merrily along on the cobblestone road until I rounded the next corner into the village, and that is when I saw several giant bulls heading straight for me. Now I understood what the farmer had been trying to tell me. The running of the bulls was taking place, and that I'd better get off the road. Next to the street was a seven-foot wall, and I don't know how I did it, but I was on top of that wall in less than a second as the angry bulls rushed past me. The villagers applauded my efforts to get out of the way of the charging bulls, and I was very happy to live another day.

It was during the summer of my second year with DoDDS when our principal, Jack Richards, suddenly came down with a case of appendicitis and was hospitalized for a couple of weeks. Unfortunately, it was just before school opened and we had no master schedule. Our assistant principal, Gene Merillo, was new to administration, and at that time, he hadn't the slightest idea how to do a master schedule. Although I had never constructed one, I volunteered to try it. Sitting at my kitchen table with 3x5 cards, I organized the classes and the times of the day that the classes would be offered. I had a card for each student in the school and I placed them into the classes that they had chosen. Although it took twenty-four hours without sleep to complete the job, we now had a master schedule. When the first day of school opened, Gene and I walked around the building and every student was in a class. My master schedule had worked and the two of us quietly danced an Irish jig and a quiet cheer for my successful efforts

Lisbon

While being groomed for an administrative position, I attended various meetings and workshops at our DoDDS headquarters in Madrid, Spain. On the way, I had a three-day layover in Lisbon, Portugal where good food and places to tour were abundant. Walking around the streets and mysterious back alleys of Lisbon, I viewed the Salazar Bridge, an exact duplicate of the Golden Gate Bridge in San Francisco, and explored the colorful districts of Castelo, Alfama, and the Barrio Alto.

One warm evening, I took the streetcar up a very steep hill, and after getting to the top of the incline, I stayed on the car and waited for the passengers to board the tram before heading back down the hill. A young man got on the streetcar and plopped down right next to me on the nearly vacant trolley. A minute went by before he shifted to his left, and his body was now pressed against mine. I began to wonder what was wrong with the guy, so I shifted to the right to get away from his full body press. Then out of nowhere, two men leaped on to the car and headed straight for the fellow sitting beside me. Now facing us, they said something to me then started punching him. I told the men to leave the kid alone, and they stopped swinging long enough to say a few things about the guy they were hitting, but I didn't understand a word of Portuguese. Two minutes later, a couple of big African fellows unceremoniously threw the two ruffians off the trolley car and the driver started back down the hill. The two assailants pursued us on foot as we sped to the bottom of the incline. Once we stopped, I shoved the guy out of the side door and motioned for him to start running, but for some reason, he wanted to stay with me. That is when I pushed him a couple of times and told him to get the hell out of here. Finally, he understood and sprinted off into the night. Who the hell did he think I was anyway, Clint Eastwood?

Madrid

The following day, I took a plane to Madrid, and after a landing that we all walked away from, I went into the passport section to go through the customs line. Because I had to take a leak, I looked for the nearest restroom, but none was to be found on this side of the customs desk. While standing in the line, I nervously paced back and forth hoping to keep from pissing in my khaki pants and making a mess out of myself. Staring at me was an alert security agent who immediately profiled me as a possible security threat. He walked over to where I was standing and politely directed me to a room on the left hand side of the terminal. I guess I could see his point. There I was, a guy wearing a beret and sporting a black mustache nervously stomping around the airport customs section. After we got to the interrogation room, he grabbed my suitcase, the one with the Penn State sticker on it, and opened it. After searching through the luggage, he felt along the lining of the case to see if I was hiding anything. Finally, after twenty minutes of questioning and searching, he let me return to the passport line. Once I checked through customs, I rushed to the men's room to relieve myself.

After a week of meetings at the DoDDS headquarters at Torrejon Air Base, I took a bus trip to the ancient town of Segovia. The city of 55,000 people, located 3000 feet above sea level on the plains of Old Castile and it proved to be well worth the two-hour trip. The sight of the picturesque city, with its ceramic red-tiled roofs resting on the top of each of its colorful buildings was stunning. Walking on the cobblestone streets, I looked up and witnessed white storks flying from one church steeple to the other pitying the poor people below who didn't have that luxury. Some of the old buildings in the City of Victory were constructed at the end of the middle-ages when the Jewish population contributed greatly to the textile industry. However, all good things came to a end when the Jews and the Moors were expelled from Spain in the final decade of the fourteenth century. Besides the Alcazar of Segovia and the San Andres Gate, another site that was impossible to overlook was the Roman aqueduct. The water carrying system was built sometime between the first and second century by placing 25,000 granite blocks held together without the use of mortar. The aqueduct had more than 170 arches and was approximately 818 square meters in length, and in its ancient splendor, the aqueduct watched over the city like a loyal guard dog. Someday, I would like to go back to Segovia, but the next time, I'll take Chieko-san with me.

During the day, our time was filled with meetings, but at night, along with a group of friends, we'd go *tapas* hopping in Madrid. For a couple of hours, we went from one bar tasting *croquestas,* and to another relishing *calamares* until it was time for dinner around eleven o'clock. We were in our final *tapas* place for the evening, where a box-like instrument, that sounded something like an accordion, was playing a bunch of romantic tunes. A guy wearing a clown suit was pumping music out of the thing when a fairly good-looking redhead approached and asked me to dance. As we were prancing around the floor, about midway through the song, I began noticing a slight lump in the Adam's apple area of her throat. I also saw that her shoulders were a little large for a woman. Suddenly it dawned on me that she wasn't a woman at all. The fact was that I was holding a man in my arms. After I finished dancing with the guy, I walked over to my grinning friends and remarked, "At least I can honestly say to my wife that I didn't dance with a woman while I was in Madrid!"

After I finished having a final mushroom, we left the bohemian place and went to a crowded restaurant on the Plaza Mayor where the diners sat at long tables and benches with their backs against each other for support. Sitting on the other side of my back was a very nice looking young woman. The slim brunette passed over her pretty shoulder a bottle of red wine whenever I needed a refill. The owner of the restaurant fancied himself a good singer, but the truth was that he wasn't half bad. He was all bad! Nevertheless, he was entertaining as he belted out, "I Left My Heart In San Francisco." He didn't sound at all like Tony Bennett, and furthermore, he was a half note off-key, but he sure knew how to have a good time.

Germany

An experience that will remain with me, until pigs learn to fly, was our 1983 summer vacation in Germany. Included in our plans was a short stay at Berchtesgaden's General Walker Hotel, located just two kilometers down the mountain from Hitler's Eagles Nest. After landing in Frankfurt, we rented a car and made our way to Dachau to see the concentration camp where thousands of souls surrendered their lives to the fascists. The forsaken victims made the earth sacred by the memories of the battered spirits they left behind. As if the ovens were still burning the bodies of the dead, the smell of leaking gas still leaked from its rusty pipes. Mitchell, Daniel, and I walked through the grounds of the camp to view the prisoners and guards quarters where our feelings were both sobering and reflective. As we were departing Dachau, just outside the camp, some Germans were laughing and digging in the muddy field that surrounded that godforsaken place. It wasn't a good laugh, and I'll never forget the looks on their grinning faces as they dug into the black German soil.

Our last stop before reaching Berchtesgaden was Rosenheim, a city with a brutal Nazi history. On 9 November 1938, the city leaders took advantage of the opportunity to deal a final blow to its Jewish citizens when a Polish Jew living in Paris, Herschel Grynzspan, walked into the German embassy and assassinated a German diplomat, Ernst von Rath. In retaliation for the crime, the SA (Storm Troopers), and hundreds of Nazis furiously attacked the Jews and closed down the town's last two remaining Jewish shops. It was known as the "Night of Glass," or *Kristallnacht*. Most of the Jews fled Rosenheim, and those who qualified, immigrated to other countries. Those who didn't have the money, or didn't believe that things where as bad as they would become, remained in Rosenheim to await their fate.

When we first got to the town, we went to a hotel, but found it to be too expensive for our budget. As we were pulling out of the parking lot, two German women sitting in a Mercedes, pulled up next to our car and asked, *Sie suchen ein Zimmer?* I replied that we were in need of a room for the night. We followed the two women to a neighborhood on the outskirts of town where their bed and breakfast inn was located. The room turned out to be neat and comfortable, so we took it for the night. A little later that evening, although it was raining cats and dogs outside, we decided to go out to have a bite to eat. Thinking that Mitchell was paying attention to the landmarks, we drove around town until we saw what appeared to be a bar that probably served food. I told the boys to wait in the car while I checked it out.

Once known for its liberalism, the city was still haunted by Nazis thugs, and I was about to come face-to-face with that execrable truth. As I walked up the steps of the bar, I heard music coming from inside the place. Singing Wehrmacht marching songs, the men were having a good time stomping their feet as they were bellowing out the music. In front of the door were two big thugs blocking my way into the tavern, so I kept my mouth shut then turned around and walked back down the wooden steps and climbed back into my car. There was no way in hell that I wanted to tangle with a couple of huge Germans. We drove around and found a restaurant that wasn't so blatantly Nazi. After finishing our dinner, we got back into our car and headed back to our inn, but quickly discovered that we were hopelessly lost. With great trepidation, after realizing that Mitchell had no idea where we were going, I went to the local police station. Like most police stations in Germany, the place reminded me of its Gestapo past, so it was very unnerving to me. After explaining my problem to a couple of the policemen, one of the cops figured out where we were staying and led us back to our bed and breakfast place.

The next morning, after a delicious breakfast of eggs, sausage, cheese, toast, and coffee, we drove on to picturesque Berchtesgaden for a few days. The village was surrounded by mountains and evergreen trees, and Hitler's Eagles Nest was perched, like an eagle, on the top of the mountain. The rooms at the General Walker Hotel were dark and redolent of the time when it was first built for high-ranking officials. When the Germans managed the hotel, it was called the *Platterhof,* where gala affairs were held. Not only was the hotel long outdated, it echoed its Nazi past. The rooms were cold, and appeared almost empty in spite of the old furniture scattered about the place. As for the weather, it was the chilliest summer I had ever experienced.

On the second day of our vacation, we drove down the mountain to Salzburg to see the sights of that picturesque city. Unfortunately, that is when the brakes went out in my car. It took a bit of luck and skill to keep the damn thing from going off the road and crashing into the pine trees, but somehow, I continued to drive slowly into Salzburg where I found a garage to repair the torn cable. While waiting for the car to be fixed, we walked around town to see the Old Town, the fortress, the cathedral, and Petersfredhof, a place were the patrician families of Saltzburg were buried. During our tour of the town, we also saw a few of the places that were featured in the movie, *The Sound of Music.*

Sicily and Italy

After two years of running the hills, enjoying the people, and counseling high school students, it was time to leave the quaint villages, the *alcatra* with *pomme frits*, and the stone-fenced farms of the Azores for a much larger island. The powers-to-be in Madrid believed that I was ready to become the new assistant principal at Sicily's Sigonella High School.

Flying to Germany at the beginning of the summer vacation, Chieko and I bought a second hand Mercedes then made our way down to the rock that the boot of Italy was kicking. We saw several historical sights along the way, including a town where the locals remembered the men of the Japanese-American 442nd infantry battalion. When we got to the Tyrrhenian Sea, we boarded a ferry at Villa San Giovanni and sailed across the strait to Messina, Sicily. From there, the two of us drove through what seemed like a hundred mountain tunnels before beginning our search for Sigonella. It wasn't anywhere on the map that I purchased at a gas station, and after searching for the naval base for two hours, we finally got some help from an old guy in a very slow-moving pickup truck. About an hour later, the Sicilian finally led us to Sigonella Naval Base. Once there, we checked into a room at the Sigonella Inn, just across the street from the main gate. After unpacking our bags, we drove onto the base to look at our new school. At the time, it was being partially renovated, so there were men and construction equipment scattered about the school grounds. Accompanied by the sound of drilling and pounding, Chieko and I stepped through a hole in the wall that led into the principal's office of the Sigonella American School.

He was writing some notes when, through the dust and debris, we got our first view of my new principal.

"Hello there. I'm Harvey Getz, and this is my wife, Chieko. I'm your new assistant principal."

The man who I later learned was a true Renaissance man who spoke French, Italian, and Czech, and was an extremely gifted painter, looked up from his papers with a quizzical look on his handsome face. After managing to surprise him, he got up from his desk to greet us. The combat veteran of Normandy, who lost his right arm to a German artillery shell at St. Lo while bending down to pick up a candy bar, was wearing an Armani shirt, stylish trousers, and a pair of loafers without socks.

"I had no idea you were going to be my assistant principal. The people in Madrid never told me," said the slim administrator. He extended his left hand out to shake my hand, "I'm Emile Mika, and it is a surprise and a pleasure to meet you and Mrs. Getz. Please excuse the mess. As you can see, they are renovating this part of building," he explained.

We talked for about thirty minutes before the unscheduled meeting came to a close. After our impromptu meeting, we drove back to the hotel for another cappuccino. Once we finished sipping our coffee, we went up to our room to relax and look over the balcony at the bobbing heads of the people in the swimming pool. An hour later, Emile Mika came over to the Sigonella Inn for some coffee and to talk about the school and what my role might be. A little later, Chieko and I ate dinner and then went back up to our room for a good night's sleep. The next morning, we returned to the school to meet with a couple of the secretaries and the administrative assistant. After spending two days at Sigonella, we left our car on the naval base and took a commercial flight back to the Azores.

We said our farewells to our friends in the Azores, then we flew to Los Angeles for ten days at my parents' apartment where I swam in the poor, went to Starbucks on La Brea, and shopped at the Beverly Shopping Center. Later in the summer, we went to Sacramento to visit with our sons, Mitchell and Daniel. We also traveled to Napa where we stayed at Lou Dawson's house for a week. While at his place, I ran the hills and valleys of that wine-producing town with my old running buddies.

During our stay in Napa, we went to Travis Air Force Base to arrange for transportation to Sicily. A sergeant at the transportation counter said that the route to Sicily was to fly to Naples and then take an air force bus to Sigonella. I explained that Naples was about eight hours away from Sicily. I also told him there was a major airport in Catania, just ten miles from the naval base. Ignoring my protests, the sergeant in charge of distributing tickets insisted that his way was the only way to get to Sicily.

That is when I asked to see his commanding officer. The captain agreed with me, and I was issued tickets to fly to Sicily.

After landing in Catania, we took a cab out to the naval base where we had parked our car a month earlier. Fortunately, the car started right up and we drove over to the hotel. Entering the parking lot of the Sigonella Inn, I saw a friend of mine who was also new to Sigonella American School. Walking beside him were his two young sons.

"Bill Fisk. What the hell are you doing here?" I shouted.

"Harv. How are you guys? It's really great to see you folks. I'm here as the new counselor," he answered.

"How can you be the new counselor? I am the new counselor," I lied.

He looked puzzled, and a look of concern crossed his handsome face. "Jezus," he said, "they must have messed up and sent us both here."

I let him worry for another couple of minutes before telling him, "Bill, I hate to tell you this, but I'm here as the new assistant principal, not as a counselor."

He sighed as a look of relief spread across his once worried face, "Man, you really got me on that one!" He declared.

The Fisk and the Getz families spent the next five weeks at the hotel sipping cappuccinos, exploring the city of Catania, and eating some fabulous meals cooked in a small coffee pot by Chieko. Although the boys sometimes gave her a hard time, Michelle watched over the two youngsters when we went into Catania. While Bill and I were at school, one of the male workers, a red-headed fellow who worked at the hotel, would often have coffee with Sandi and Chieko and talk about nothing important. The two women referred to him as "the pimp."

At the beginning of the year, my new position as assistant principal was a bit confusing, mainly because I didn't know what the principal expected of me. But a week after the school year began, the situation was clarified when Mr. Mika called the two assistant principals into his office and assigned us our duties. The other assistant principal, Dwight Wainwright, was put in charge of the elementary school annex as well as ordering the supplies for the school. My assignment was to remain in the main building assisting the principal in all duties necessary for running the school. Additionally, I was given the task of ordering next year's supplies for the high school. Two weeks later, when I went to Emile to make a decision on a matter that I've long since forgotten, he responded, "If you need to ask me whether you can do something, then I don't need you." I finally understood what Mr. Mika expected from me. From that time on, I made decisions based on what I thought was the best for the school. Not once did my principal ever second guess me or question my intentions to make the school a better place for everyone.

After sleeping his way through the year, the assistant principal at the elementary school ignored the principal's directive to order the supplies. Left with no other choice, I ordered the supplies for the elementary school.

Emile and his wife, Ellie, lived in a lovely apartment full of paintings and artifacts. Residing just a few blocks from us in Catania, it wasn't long before we became friends and commuted together. Emile, my son, Daniel, and I, would stop midway during our ten-mile commute for a cappuccino and a cornetto at a cafe next to the highway. Meeting us there every morning were three teachers, Jane Bratkowski, Terry Anderson, and her husband, Harry. After enjoying a few laughs, the six of us continued on our way to Sigonella. When school was over for the day, Emile and I would have our sponge activity, a phrase borrowed from the Effective Teaching Program. It meant finding something that is usually not part of the lesson, but continuing with that topic for a while. Anyway, our sponge activity was going to a cafe after work to enjoy a cup of coffee together. Emile had his favorite place, and I had my preferred bar. Quite often, especially when we were having a really good time, we ended up going to both places.

Ellie Mika had an encounter on the streets of Catania when a thief ripped a gold chain from her lovely neck. Ellie had trepidations about going back outside onto the streets of Catania alone, but she gradually overcame them and went out to do some shopping. We were at one of Emile's coffee bars when the principal glanced at his watch for the fourth time in the last ten minutes. He was worried about his wife.

"I wonder where Ellie is? She was supposed to meet us at five o'clock here at the coffee bar. It's almost five-thirty," he sighed.

Emile and Ellie visited the bar quite often, so the bartender considered the couple to be his friends. If you were friends of a Sicilian, there was nothing he or she would hesitate to do for you. But if you weren't, you were strictly on you own. Walking to the other end of the bar, the bartender picked up the phone and made a call. Two minutes later, the gentleman walked back to Emile.

"Your wife is standing in front of Rinocente Department Store. She is perfectly fine," he announced.

The Mafia was keeping an eye on Ellie Mika. The swarthy band of gangsters wanted to ensure that no one would ever bother her again while on the streets of Catania.

Christmas was just around the corner when the faculty was throwing a dinner party at a restaurant located somewhere near Siracusa. The four of us were in Emile's BMW looking for the elusive place, but we were having a hell of a time finding it. We stopped at a couple of gas stations, but they didn't have any idea where the restaurant might be. As the saying goes, time waits for no one. Even if we eventually found the place, we were already over an hour late. Finally admitting defeat, we had to come up with some excuse that the faculty might believe.

"This won't do," cried Emile. "The principal and the assistant principal, the school's leaders, can't even find the bloody restaurant! Harv, what are we going to do?"

"I've got an idea, I replied. "How can it be that two administrators are unable to find the restaurant, especially since everybody else on our staff found the place? Well, I say we tell them that while on the way to the restaurant when were held up by robbers."

Through the windows of Emile's car, his laugh was loud enough to be heard a half a block away.

"That's brilliant, absolutely brilliant. We'll say that we were held up at gun point and all our money was taken from our wallets," Emile laughed.

"Yes, the 'we wiz robbed routine' just might work. That is if all of us pledge to never tell the truth," I added.

The four of us swore an oath of allegiance to never tell the faculty what really happened. The following day, we broke the news about our "robbery."

"Holy cow!" Exclaimed Katy Ailes, "I feel really bad for you guys. It must have been awful."

"My God! Are you guys all right?" Cried Andy Cano.

"Jezus, are the women OK?" Mike Summers asked.

I would say that everything worked out pretty well for us. We received sympathetic comments instead of the scorn we would have received if we had told them that the two leaders of the school couldn't find the restaurant.

It was in early June when the school was holding the Class of 1985 graduation ceremony at the floral-laden grounds of the University of Catania. Emile was dressed in an Armani suit, and I was wearing my white jacket and blue trousers, and both of us added a small bit of dignity to the occasion. Sitting at the very front row of the outdoor stage, we were feeling very pleased with ourselves that everything was going well. However, when the principal and assistant principal of Sigonella Schools were involved, happiness had its risks, because when we were satisfied with ourselves, we had the tendency to throw caution out the window. For example, when Mike Summers and his girlfriend arrived at the ceremony, I said, "Here comes Mike Summers and that flamboyant dance hall singer of his!" A few minutes later, it was time for Bill Fisk, our guidance counselor, who was dressed in a white suit, to say a few words to our graduates, honored guests, and friends. After getting up on the stage to speak, we noticed that his fly was wide open. Unaware that anything was wrong, he continued speaking while we did our best not laugh our skinny asses off. But we failed miserably.

Our high school band played a song following Bill's speech, and as the number was coming to a close, I leaped up on the stage and thanked them for that great introduction.

After the ceremony was over, we had a few drinks at the university lounge where Emile told Bill that his fly was down. Without comment, Bill Fisk immediately zipped it up.

Although I seldom competed anymore, running was still an important part of my life. I'd jog around town every morning around four-thirty hoping that I wouldn't blunder onto a Mafia killing somewhere on the backstreets of the city. The morning sun had yet to shine her light on the city when I spotted a couple of cars with hairy looking guys parked in front of the Palace of Justice. I glanced over at them, and they returned my look with their evil eyes. Turning quickly away from their stares, I picked up my pace hoping like hell they wouldn't chase me down the street and plug me full of holes. Thankfully, they didn't, but a few hours later, on my way to school, I saw policemen with automatic weapons standing on nearly every corner of the city. When I got to school, I asked one of my Sicilian friends if he knew what was happening in Catania that morning. Reitano, the school's administrative assistant, said that a police roundup of corrupt judges was taking place, and the men I saw in the parked cars were former Mafia guys now working for the police.

Chieko and I drove up into the mountains of Sicily to visit Piazza Armerina, an old Roman army recreation center that was famous for its ancient mosaics. Not far from the site, we spotted a cafe and decided to stop for a leisurely lunch. As we walked into the restaurant, there was only one other couple in the place, and it was as quiet as a mouse in a cat's cage. In fact, the place was so empty that an echo bounced off the walls every time we spoke. After having our choice of tables, we selected one by a window and sat down to enjoy an excellent meal of a salad, chicken, and pasta, and we washed it down with a pleasant glass of red wine. Not long after we had placed our order, the two other customers finished eating, then they leisurely paid their bill and departed from the restaurant. After they left, I asked the proprietor, "Would you mind if I bring in a tape player so we can play some Edith Piaf?"

"Of course not. That would be very nice," he replied.

It was a sunny but a refreshingly cool afternoon as we slowly ate our meal and listened to Piaf sing, "La Vie En Rose." The birds outside were chirping with a bit of humor, and the flowers that surrounded the restaurant were in full bloom. We were at peace with the world, and our hearts were warmed by the sheer loveliness of the setting. Suddenly, we looked up and saw the owner, and a policeman, who had just entered the restaurant, loading their shotguns and closing the shutters.

"The Mafia is coming!" Shouted the owner.

"Holy cow! The Mafia is coming. Chieko, we gotta' get out here right now!" I shouted.

Quickly shutting off Edith Piaf in the middle of "Le Vagabond," I left some money on the table, then Chieko and I quickly exited the restaurant by climbing through one of the windows that still hadn't been boarded up. We rushed to our car only to discover the driveway was blocked by a couple of other automobiles. Left with no choice, we drove through the shrubbery and high tailed it out of there. Speeding down the road, well above the speed limit, we laughed in the face of our possible demise. No doubt about it, the escape from the Mafia added to the romance of the afternoon.

On a side street in Catania, while waiting for the red light to change, we noticed a bus in front of us jammed with passengers looking out the windows at the people walking by. What we didn't see was that a couple of would-be thieves pulled up beside us on their motorcycle. Having lived in the city for a couple of years, one of the things that we learned to do was secure Chieko's purse to the gear shift just in case some bad guys tried to steal it. I was in the middle of a conversation when I noticed that Chieko wasn't answering me. I looked over at my wife and I saw an ugly fellow laying next to her trying to unwrap the purse from the gearshift. She was holding on to the purse with one hand, while he was kicking her other arm that was holding onto the door. Because she kept the door from opening all the way, he couldn't get his whole body into the car. Chieko was wearing her thick leather coat, and without it, she would have felt the sting of his vicious kicks. When I saw what he was trying to do, I reached over and placed my hand over his, then pulled back his fingers causing him to scream with pain. I reached over with my other hand to smash him in the face, but my seat belt prevented me from reaching my target. Frustrated by the completely silent resistance, he yelled, *Bursa! Bursa!* He wanted the purse, but no matter how hard he tried, he wasn't able to free it from the gearshift. Finally he became frustrated and suffering from a great deal of pain, he gave up his attempt then jumped out of the car and hopped onto the back of their getaway motorcycle.

"Yea," I shouted. "The Getz family 1. Ladri 0."

A few months later, the bad guys evened the score when I was pick-pocketed at the Catania fish market. Fortunately, another thing that I had learned to do was not to carry a wallet while walking in the city. Instead, I only carried enough money in my plastic traveler's check holder to buy a shirt at one of the stores.

Life is, indeed, elliptical. This phenomenon led us to reacquainting ourselves with a woman I briefly met many years ago in Tokyo. Fifteen years had passed since I last spoke to the Japanese woman in the cab bound for the Tokyo Airport. The young woman planned to continue her operatic studies in Milan, Italy, but it was destiny that made us to run into her again at the Sicilian fish market. While looking at a giant chunk of raw tuna, Sakamoto-san, in Japanese, asked, "Do you think that it is good *sashimi?*" That culinary question was the beginning of our relationship with the opera star who was appearing as *Madame Butterfly* at the Catania Opera House. After Sakamoto-san became friends with Chieko, she mentioned that she liked the way my wife fixed her own hair. The opera star asked Chieko to make up her hair for the remainder of her performances of *Madame Butterfly* at the opera house.

We made friends with a Ouija board spirit who showed up on Friday nights whenever Jean Bratkowski, a fellow teacher, was at the sessions. We speculated that "David" must have liked her because he responded to nearly all of her questions without hesitation. Jean asked if this was the year that she was going to get a transfer? The spirit replied, "Yes."

We asked where the transfer was going to be? The spirit replied with a collection of letters that made no sense to us. Later in the year, we learned that the letters were a combination of two places; Athens and Zaragoza. Jean was offered transfers to both of those places.

Mitchell was home from the University of Santa Barbara for the winter vacation, and he was having good time mocking us as we maneuvered our way on the Ouija board. After having a few laughs at our expense, we dared him to take a place at the board. When he sat down and placed his hands on the Ouija board, it went bananas. The triangular apparatus went up and down and across the board in what appeared to be a fit of anger. I eased Mitchell out of his seat and got back on the board with Jean. I asked the spirit to please forgive Mitchell because he was young and foolish and that he didn't know any better. Finally, after a few minutes of running back and forth on the board, the spirit forgave Mitchell, and all of us breathed a collective sigh of relief.

Emile Mika praised my efforts in administration, and expressed the opinion that I was ready to become a principal at every opportunity. The powers in Madrid finally believed him and they finally decided to promote me. However, if I could push a button and go back in time, I would choose to repeat my two years as assistant principal at Sigonella High School. Emile was my principal and best friend, and it was an honor and a privilege to work with a man with such integrity, honesty, and talent.

Gaeta, Italy

Driving from Sigonella to Messina, then after a short ferryboat ride across the Strait of Messina, we drove up the peninsula for another four hours while singing the Beatles hit, "We Don't Live In A Yellow Submarine." On the way to Gaeta, the site of my new school, Michelle noticed that our cat, Sophio, who we adopted in Sicily, was missing. We looked everywhere for our pet, but he was nowhere to be found. At a food stop a few kilometers back, we purchased some items for our temporary apartment but Sophio was locked in the car, so there wasn't any chance for him to escape. After searching everywhere in the car, Daniel happened to look in the bag of groceries. Alas! There was the cat sleeping on top of the frozen bacon that we bought at the market. Our automobile that we had purchased in Germany didn't have air conditioning, and that was the coolest spot the overheated cat could find.

Gaeta was an enchantingly beautiful city with an abundance of places to see and a myriad of things to do. Included among the sites was the prison where Herbert Kappler, the former Gestapo chief and architect of Rome's Ardeatine massacre was imprisoned. The SS officer became ill with cancer and was subsequently moved to a hospital in Rome. A short time later, his wife stuffed the now skinny Obersturmbahnfuher in a suitcase, and the two Nazis escaped to Germany to live out the remainder of their days.

There are those who believed that the picturesque town was one of the Department of Defense Schools best kept secrets. It featured churches, old medieval quarters, a wonderful beach, and a host of outdoor restaurants that lined the street adjacent to the sea. At those restaurants, vacationers from Rome and Naples ate and drank to the sounds of strumming guitars, screaming vocalists, and pounding drums.

The walk to the sandy beach from our temporary apartment was only five minutes away, so it was easy for me to take refreshing swims in the Mediterranean Sea and gawk at the lovely women.

The evenings were equally pleasant. The four of us would dine on the veranda of our apartment and watch the people out for their evening *passeggio*. After eating, we would also go for a walk and listen to the potpourri of music from the various outdoor restaurants. However, the carefree times ended when we found a large and beautiful house in the nearby town of Formia, that was located next to the Tyrrhenian Sea. Surrounded by a beautiful garden full of flowers and vegetables, except for the owner of the house, everybody had to keep their mitts of the flora. The attractive brick house, with a large back porch, was located on a very quiet street where our cat learned to bark from a very noisy dog that lived next door to us. The proprietor stayed in half the large basement when he wasn't at his Naples home, while Daniel roomed in the other half of the subterranean room that doubled as his bedroom and music studio. Taking up the guitar when we lived in Catania, it wasn't long before Dan was singing and playing gigs in the clubs around Naples. Michelle found a job with NATO in Naples, and was doing extremely well as one of the admiral's secretaries.

A good night's sleep was something that Daniel rarely enjoyed. The student, musician, and soccer player got up every morning at four-thirty to catch the school bus to Naples where he attended Naples High School. His soccer practices and evening gigs in Naples cut into his limited slumber time leaving Daniel somewhat sleep deprived.

Daniel's girlfriend, Katrina, and her sister, were visiting him from Sigonella when they decided to take out the Ouija board to see if they could reach a spirit. A few minutes later, they found themselves communicating with someone from the other world. They learned that a young girl was haunting our house, and that she was willing to answer most of their questions. When asked what language she spoke, the spirit responded in Italian, *tutti,* all languages. One of the questions that Katrina asked was, "Am I going to pass algebra this year?" The spirit replied that she would barely pass the class, but she would pass it. The spirit also knew the name of our cat, and that she was very fond of Sophio. The password that Daniel and the girls shared during the Libyan crises to get to their house past the security police wasn't a secret as far as the spirit was concerned. She accurately disclosed that it was, "Romeo and Juliette."

When Daniel asked what happened to her, the spirit replied that she was killed in the war.

At the kindergarten through grade eight school, our secretary, Anna Napolitano, was very efficient and competent, and like most Italians, a true coffee lover. Although I had already finished a cappuccino earlier in the morning, at nine o'clock she would order two cappuccinos from the bar across the street. Together, we would drink our coffee, and then it was back to work until noon. At twelve o'clock, we would go over to the bar for a panini and another cappuccino. At two o'clock, she would order espressos for the two of us. Anna was a good person, but she sure drank a lot of coffee. And so did I.

At the DoDDS administrators' conference in Livorno, several principals brought their wives to enjoy the friendship that was a part of those meetings. The women managed their time wisely by touring Pisa with its leaning tower, the Piazza dei Cavalier, and the Borgo Stretto. Chieko and the group of women also went to Firenze (Florence) for the day to do some shopping and stroll around the baroque piazzas. After they got off the train, the entourage began their trek into the middle of the city. However, on the way, they were confronted by a group of gypsies that were hell bent on robbing the seemingly well-to-do women. Just as they were making their final approach to strip the ladies of their prized possessions, Chieko punched one of the girls on the top of her head. The angry girls chased the Americans down a narrow street, but the women escaped by ducking into an exclusive shop. Because the gypsies weren't permitted to enter the store, they gave up their chase and left the women to enjoy the rest of the day in Firenze.

People who have strong personalities have a way of effecting those around them, either in a good or a bad way. One fellow who had a positive impact on me was Rino Agosti. The former professional soccer star from the famous Naples team, deep-sea diver, sea captain, and supply clerk, was a man who loved his wife, children, his land, and even his mother-in-law. Chieko and I, on a couple of occasions, were invited to his mountainside home to partake in a few of his brides scrumptious dinners washed down by a plethora of vino. Everything that Signora Agosti prepared was freshly home grown. The wine, sausages, olives, pasta, and tomatoes were all from the fertile land that surrounded their house. While at the Agosti's home, we didn't eat. We feasted!

Soccer had been kind to Rino Agosti. When he was a kid, he was sent to live with a coach in Milano where he went to school and played European football everyday. Eventually, he was promoted up through the ranks and ended up on the great Naples team. The years rolled by for the former football player, and now he was our logistic's man at Gaeta Elementary School. Occasionally, amateur football teams would call on him to play for them whenever they were short a man. The US Navy guys would laugh when they saw him come out on the field. Rino sported a fairly healthy gut, and didn't look much like a soccer player anymore, but they stopped laughing when he skillfully dribbled past all the opponents to score a goal.

Rino was the kind of fellow that if you needed anything, he would do his best to get it for you--no matter what it was. Supply records where a bit foreign to Rino, but he was always aware what was in stock and he ordered the items whenever they were in short supply. One day, I asked him to arrange a tour of Monte Cassino for the staff, and he did so with dispatch. The old monastery was founded in AD 529 by the Benedict of Nursia, and in 1944, it was the site of a five-month battleground between the Allies and the Germans. In the battle for the Monte Cassino, 55,000 allied and 20,000 German troops were killed or injured before the German paratroopers finally surrendered the monastery to the Polish forces.

After getting off the rented bus, arranged by Rino Agosti, the head priest walked arm-in-arm with Chieko and I around the grounds of the abbey. The three of us stood in the exact spot where the priest was standing when the bombs from the American B-17's were dropped on Monte Casino. A diffused bomb, that landed as a dud, rested just a few feet away from where the three of us stood. By giving the Germans rubble to hide behind, it was even more difficult for the allies to capture the monastery. Later, the priest took Chieko and I into their private library where thousands of books where being translated from Latin into Italian. Tacked onto a cabinet door, we were amazed to see the very first translated document. While in the library, I held the original *Dante's Inferno* in my trembling hands. The book had notes in the margins written by Dante's son. As the translator of the arts and humanities, according to the head priest, they still had a thousand more years of work to do.

An intentional mistake that I made every Saturday as our train pulled in the Rome railroad station was cry, *"Finamente! Bella Napoli."* Finally!

Beautiful Naples. People would look at me strangely, and then come to the following conclusion: *Poor fellow. He thinks he is in Naples. I guess he got on the wrong side of the tracks and took the Rome train instead of the one to Naples.* Chieko would sometimes laugh, but after saying it a half a dozen times it got to be a little old, but I continued saying it anyway. One day, while we were on the train to Rome, I started talking to a British kid about going to Naples today. He asked some questions about Naples and mentioned that he couldn't wait to see the sights. I thought to myself, *this fellow plays the game better than I do.* Some of the places that he planned to see were the Piazza del Plebiscito, and the Villa Comunale Park. We continued lying to each other until I finally realized that he wasn't kidding. I'll be damned if he didn't think that we really were going to Naples. I finally came out with the truth and told him that we were going to Rome, not Naples.

"Dammit! I'm on the wrong bloody train." He asked, "What should I do?"

I said to the exasperated traveler, "Relax. Just get off at the next stop and walk to the other side of the tracks. There will be a train going to Naples shortly."

The young man thanked me several times before getting off at the next stop. However, that didn't stop me from continuing to play my favorite mind game every time we went to Rome.

During our weekend trips to Rome, among the places we visited were the Colosseum, the monument to Vittorio Emanuele II (sometimes called the birthday cake), St. Peter's Basilica, the Trevi Fountain, and many other sites. One Sunday afternoon, while walking down *via Veneto*, we were suddenly surrounded by a group of prowling gypsies. As they were making their final approach, a bartender ran out of his place and kicked their gypsy butts all the way down the block. We graciously thanked the man for his kind assistance, then continued on our way to the Spanish Steps.

Many years had gone by since Betty Johnson, the former principal at Landstuhl Junior High School allegedly made her crack about Hitler not killing enough Jews. I was an assistant principal at Sigonella when I learned from our regional director that the former Betty Johnson was now Betty Alberghetti. The woman had a name change after she married a much younger Italian man. When I heard this from the DoDDS director, I laughed and said that he'd better not put me within a hundred miles of her because I might strangle her. Well, as it turned out, she was the principal of Naples Elementary School, and my coordinating principal. The first time she called me, it took all my patience not to say anything about her long-ago indiscretion. Apparently, she had completely forgotten about it, and I began to think that I should too. Eventually, we learned to tolerate each other and we became acquaintances. About a year after she retired, while Chieko and I were having dinner at their place in Gaeta, she said, "Harv, let me give you a piece of advice, don't ever retire. Retirement stinks!"

Six months after arriving in Gaeta, I received a phone call from our assistant director who wanted to know, if asked, would I interested in transferring to Turkey. I answered, "Yes, if I have a chance to go to Turkey, I would take it." He thanked me and hung up the phone. The next day, he called back and offered me Izmir, Turkey.

Greece and Turkey

Bidding farewell to Rino Agosti, Anna Napolitano, and the rest of the staff, we climbed into our car and we were off for yet another adventure. Our first stop was Brindisi, where we boarded a crowded ferryboat bound for Piraeus, Greece. Although the ride across the Ionian Sea was a bit rough, with a little help from a bottle of wine, we weathered the storm. After touring the ship and having a bite to eat, we settled into our cramped sleeping quarters for the evening. Following a fairly restless night, we drove our car off the ferry in Piraeus and went into Athens to check into a room at the Apollon Hotel. For a couple of days we walked the ancient streets, traveled across its wide boulevards, and walked to the Parthenon to view the ancient crumbling structure. In a small shop near the Acropolis, Chieko was charmed into buying a green fur coat from a guy named George. During our evenings in Athens, we ate at a couple of Greek dinners, but I refrained from the traditional tossing of our dirty dishes against the wall.

Our two days in Athens were wonderful, but it was time to continue our journey on to Turkey. On the third morning, we left the hotel to begin our drive to the Greek-Turkish border. After driving for two hours, it was getting close to noon, so we stopped at a road-side restaurant for lunch, and somewhere in that busy restaurant, there was a guy who wanted us dead.

Ten minutes after we left the restaurant, we were speeding down the two-lane highway where I was trying not be be too distracted by Greece's scenery, when I glanced at the side mirror and noticed a pickup truck weaving in and out of the traffic. He seemed to be in a really big hurry, but it wasn't long before I figured out that he was passing all the other cars to get to me. The guy passed the car behind me then he pulled up next to us. Without any warning, he suddenly swerved sharply into our traffic lane. It was at that moment that I made the life-saving decision to stay on a steady course instead of veering off the side of the road. I stepped on the gas pedal of my Mercedes and zoomed forward. After what seemed like a minute, but it was probably only a few seconds, he gave up the chase and sped down the highway just ahead of us. At the next village, the would-be assassin pulled onto a side street and he watched us as we continued on down the road.

"Wow! That was close," I cried.

"What was he trying to do?" Chieko asked.

"Kill us," I replied.

Out in the middle of nowhere was the Greek-Turkish border. The stark place reminded me of Dante's hell, or perhaps a Sergio Leone film. The surrounding area was absent of flora and fauna, and except for a guard shack, it was a vacant of all life. While at the border, in the howling wind and freezing temperature, the Greeks hassled me for approximately a half an hour. Standing out in the cold wind, I answered the same questions for what seemed like a hundred times.

"Vat are you? Who are you? Why are you going to that other country?" The guy never once said, "Turkey,"

"My name is Harvey Getz. I work for the US government. I am going to Turkey to become the president of the American School," I repeated over and over again.

One of the reasons for his concern was a week earlier, there was some shooting between the two countries at that very same border. But finally the Greeks released us, then we carefully drove about a kilometer down the road to the Turkish border. Once we were there, the Turks treated us like long-lost brothers and sisters. When I walked into their guard shack, the police greeted me warmly, then stamped our passports before waving us through the gate. Now on our way, we drove through the early evening into the first town that we came across. The city, about fifteen kilometers from the border, was called Edirne. Driving around the mid-sized town, we discovered a very pleasant hotel, and that is where we decided to spend our first night in Turkey. After unpacking our bags, we showered and changed clothes before going downstairs to dinner. The evening meal was great, and to be perfectly honest, I'd say that we had one of the best and most inexpensive meals that we had ever eaten. Included with our dinner was a bottle of succulent white wine. And to top it off, two waiters were standing by to attend to our every need

"You know, Harv, I think I'm going to like Turkey," Chieko said.

"I think I like it, already." I replied.

The next morning, while having breakfast, Michelle, with a look of utter amazement on her lovely face, came running into the breakfast room. "Come here, I want to show you guys something."

"All right. Just as soon as we finish our breakfast," I said.

"No. Come now," she insisted. "You guys have got to see this."

"All right," I said. The three of us got up from the breakfast table and followed Michelle into the next room.

In the outer room, there was a large picture window revealing a panoramic view of the activities that were happening on the street in front of the hotel. Much to my surprise, I was looking at a scene that I had only witnessed in movies of old Eastern European street scenes. The people were dressed in black baggy clothes, and they were selling such items as bread, live chickens, and various kinds of fruit. The carts they were pushing were loaded with all kinds of peppers, carrots, tomatoes, and greens of all kinds. Donkeys and horses were pulling wagons loaded with meat and other foodstuffs that were suitable for any peasant or king. It was an fascinating scene that none of us will ever forget. If I didn't know better, I could have sworn I was on the set of Barbra Streisand's, "Yentl."

On the way to Izmir, we drove through Canakkale, where the ancient battle of Troy and the World War I bloodbath of the Australians at Gallipoli took place. Our next city was Bursa, once the center of the silk trade along the Silk Road. Finally, after a couple more hours of driving, we arrived in Izmir, the town once known by its biblical name, Smyrna.

We checked into two rooms at the Cordon Hotel, then the four of us went outside to explore the town. Rich with Turkish delights, the city was comprised of mosques, small shops, shoe shine boys, the Aegean Sea, carpet stores, mysterious alleyways, and a host of fine restaurants. As for the people, they dressed in western clothes and they looked more European than Middle Eastern.

Two weeks later, we moved into a waterfront seventh story apartment, just a half-mile up the street from the hotel. While settling into our new place on the First Cordon, we had our choice of rooms, but for some strange reason, none of us chose the room with a built-in desk and bookcase. Since no one claimed the room, we made it our guest and storage room but I rarely entered the room, but when I did, I exited as quickly as possible. Even our cat managed to avoid the place. None of us said anything, but we suspected that it was haunted.

One night, Chieko was up late reading, so I went to the room to get some sleep. Settling quickly into a deep sleep, I dreamed on until the middle of the night when I was suddenly awakened by someone or something heavy sitting on my chest. In a state of sheer panic, I leaped out of the bed and rushed out of the spooky room then jumped into bed with Chieko. I pulled the covers over my head and fell into an uneasy sleep. One thing was for certain, I never stayed in that haunted room again.

All things considered, my new school proved to be a real challenge to both my intellect and my resolve. When I first arrived at the Izmir American School, over half of the staff lined up in the hallway to complain about the assistant principal. Simply put, they wanted her fired. To back up their demand, the union president came to town to meet with me and he warned me that if I didn't get rid of her, both of us would lose our jobs. There was nothing I could do about the assistant principal for the reason that she was well liked by our director. One thing I could do, however, was look out for the teachers as best I could. But there were those times when even that was hard to do. For example, while attending a meeting in Madrid, the regional director wanted me to suspend the local union president for ten days for not paying her rent in seven months. I refused to do it. "I have to live with that staff, so I'm not going to suspend her."

When I got back to Izmir, I called her into my office to discuss the matter. The teacher's excuse for not paying the rent was that it was the stress of the job that kept her from paying her bills. Although I didn't believe her, I gave her the rest of the day off to pay her rent, but she still didn't pay it.

The school was a former tobacco warehouse, and it didn't matter what improvements were made, it still looked and smelled like a warehouse. I tried to make things a little better for the staff, including air conditioning the two buildings and doubling the glass on the windows to keep out the noisy street sounds. However, these minor improvements weren't enough to change the educational environment. Since there wasn't a playground, one of the programs that I implemented was that every Friday afternoon, the kids and the teachers took a bus out to Bayrakli Park for a few hours of fun and exercise.

While I enjoyed most aspects of the city, I found the rest of Turkey exciting and mysterious. My daily runs around the city were an important part of the magic that was Turkey. When I reached the halfway mark of my run, from a nearby minaret, I would hear the *Muezzin* call out the *Adhan* for the evening prayers. When the call to prayer was sounded, the men dropped whatever they were doing and made their way to the various mosques throughout the city. Most of the people in Turkey were Sunni Moslems, but as far as I could tell, they seemed to get along pretty well with the Shia Moslems.

Atypical, as far as people were concerned, was my loyal logistic's guy. He was a very intelligent fellow named Yusuff, who could disarm both man and beast with his logic. One day, we went to a couple of local offices to get some documents approved. After going to three different places and waiting for a long time at each of the offices for service, I grew impatient. It seemed that those waiting to be helped were not as important to the office workers as smoking cigarettes and drinking tea.

I said to Yusef, "What the hell is this? Here we are sitting here patiently waiting, while the men who should be helping us, are drinking tea and smoking cigarettes."

"Yes, I know that," Yusuf replied.

"If this were in the United States, the people would rebel and the workers would be in deep kim chee," I said.

"Well, this isn't the United States. The Turkish people don't like it any better than the Americans do. But we have no choice."

"What do you mean by, "no choice?" I asked.

"Well, let me tell you a little story. One day, I came home from work and our baby boy was really sick, so we took him to a nearby hospital to see a doctor. After waiting for a couple of hours while the doctors and nurses drank their *chai* and smoked their cigarettes, I started complaining. Well, a few minutes later, a couple of policemen showed up and hauled me off to jail. I stayed there until the DoDDS Director came from Madrid to free me."

"Wow! So that is why everybody just sits here and says nothing," I said.

"Yes. That is exactly why we don't say anything," he replied.

Greece and Crete

For the second time in five years, I went to Athens and Crete to serve on the North Central Association committee responsible for recommending the accreditation of the Department of Defense Dependent Schools. Shortly after my arrival in Athens, there was a party for the team at the Apollon Hotel. About a half hour into the soiree, the superintendent of schools told our leader, a tough old geezer who was a professor from the University of Minnesota, that she was not to pay any attention to the principal. "He is on his way out," she said. "Furthermore, I am now running the school." What the superintendent revealed was a clear violation of the North Central Association code of ethics and practices. The team leader immediately called for an emergency meeting. At the meeting, we were told to keep notes on any violations of the ethics policy and report them to him. During the final evaluation meeting, I was the only guy to stand up to the team leader when he told us that he was against approving the accreditation. I argued that it was unfair to withhold accreditation because of the superintendent's actions. Finally, I convinced the gentleman to change his mind, but when we were finished evaluating the school, things didn't go that well for the superintendent.

Our trip over to Crete was aboard a luxurious Greek ferryboat. The only problem that we encountered was that a stowaway had chosen our cabin to hide out. Three of us had paid for the entire cabin and we knew that he didn't belong there. The obtrusive guy was pretending to be asleep, and the ashtray was overflowing with what was left of his cigarettes, We had to get him out of our room, so we went upstairs to complain to the fellow in charge of cabin assignments. He and a couple of other men went down to our cabin and hauled his sorry ass out of there.

After we docked, the NCA team made its way out to Heraklion Air Base and settled into our very plush quarters at the base lodge. That evening, with the smell of fennel in the air, we went out to a nearby restaurant and enjoyed a wonderful Greek salad, mizitha cheese, and roasted lamb washed down with a couple of bottles of Crete's finest wine. Everyone was in a festive mood, and we had a strong desire to do a good job with the evaluation process, while at the same time, we were going to enjoy all that Crete had to offer.

The next day, we met with the entire staff to brief them on what was going to occur over the next three days. One of the teachers that I interviewed published a list of special education students and posted it on her bulletin board. This was convenient for the teacher, but it was a clear violation of NCA standards. I was supposed to report it, but instead, I asked her to remove it without telling our illustrious leader about it.

Crete is the fifth largest island in the Mediterranean. The one hundred sixty mile long island, with its 600,000 people had the greatest number of people of all the islands. Surrounded by olive trees and citrus groves, Heraklion is the capital city. Her long history dates back to 2700 BC when Crete was the heart of Europe's first advanced civilization. I spent a couple of hours wandering around the Knossos, a crumbling structure that once was the heart of the Minoan culture. Their society was Amazonian, which meant that the women of Minoa were in charge of all aspects of their civilization. As for the men, when they outlived their usefulness, or simply became boring, they didn't wake up the next day.

We finished our evaluation and it was recommended by the committee that the Crete American School's accreditation be approved. As we were preparing to leave the island, I heard on the television that a storm was approaching and that all flights back to mainland of Greece were going to be cancelled. After watching the news, I rushed into Heraklion and booked a suite on a cruise ship that was leaving for Athens early the next morning. I told my two friends about it, a gay male and a very good looking woman. Together, they went into town and booked passage back back to Athens. Both of them stayed with me in my large suite that night.

When I got back to my school, I received a phone call from the regional director who wanted to know the facts about the district superintendent. His voice was pretty loud, but when I told him that the charges against the woman were true, his tone dropped several decibels and he thanked me before hanging up the phone.

A rather serious incident occurred during my time as principal of Izmir American School. Our host nation teacher decided that it would be educational for the elementary and high school kids to take a field trip to Manissa. All seemed to go well until that evening when there was a knock on our apartment door. When I answered the door, the host nation teacher greeted me. Surprised, but pleased to see her, I invited her into our apartment. After hesitating for a moment, she proceeded to tell me that once they had arrived in Manissa. Some of the romantically inclined high school students didn't get off the bus until they were finished making out with each other. Several Turkish men were looking through the bus window getting their jollies off while they watched the debacle. When the girls finally got off the bus, the Turks attempted to grab the girls because they thought they were prostitutes. And if that wasn't bad enough, one of the elementary students stole some prayer beads from the mosque. After hearing the report, I had a good idea who took the beads. Chieko and I jogged down the First Cordon to the colonel's apartment to inform him of the incident. I knew that there could be political implications, so there was a real sense of urgency in resolving the matter as quickly as possible. The making out on the bus would have to wait until the morning, but the issue of the beads had to resolved immediately. When I got to the Air Force colonel's quarters to tell him about the theft of the beads, he wasn't sure what to do. At that point, I suggested that he pick up the red phone that connected him to the military police and tell them to search the suspected boy's quarters. The cops paid a visit to the lad's quarters, and the beads were found. They were later returned to the mosque by Colonel Toughnick, the commanding officer of the US Army unit in Izmir. Without any time for the Turks to jail the kid, the Army colonel sent the boy and his mother back to the states on the next plane out of Izmir. As for the students who were making out on the bus, after talking to a couple of the parents who had gone on the trip to help supervise the kids, I suspended them for ten days. There was a lot of protests from their NATO fathers, but in spite of their complaints, I stuck to my decision.

The incident is still referred to as the "Manissa Massacre."

Most of my Saturday mornings were spent driving out into the countryside where I ran past an old Roman bridge and up the mountain for six miles. After reaching the top of the hill, there was a decrepit teahouse where men from the village gathered during the day to gossip while their wives farmed the nearby fields. I'd have some *chai,* and then rest for about thirty minutes before heading back down the mountain. Among the many thoughts I had was that men everywhere were much the same. We wanted our families to be safe, have good food on the table, and be healthy. Of course, we had our own cultures and traditions, but we had more things in common than the differences that defined us.

During the spring of my third year at the school, I organized a *volksmarch* up that same mountain. Taking a couple of buses to the old Roman bridge, the kindergarten through grade three students had their lunch and played until later in the afternoon when the younger students were transported up to the top of the mountain on school buses. The rest of the kids had a good time walking the entire way up the hill. When we got to the top of the mountain, along with the surprised but excited villagers, we all gathered in front of the antiquated teahouse for a concert by the school band. There we were, approximately four hundred kids and teachers dressed in red tee shirts listening to the lively concert. Just as the band was in the middle of *Alexander's Rag Time Band,* a parade of camels appeared and unexpectedly swayed between the band and the audience. When Big Ed, the band director's husband went to take a picture of his wife, Mary, directing the band with the graceful camels strutting by, he snapped the picture, but Ed discovered that his camera was out of film. In all my years as an educator, I never saw a grown man cry like that before. As the camels were moving past the band, I joked with the teachers that it had cost me five bucks to arrange the whole thing.

On several weekends, Chieko and I drove to the seaside resort of Kusadashi with our school secretary and her husband, a mathematics teacher at our school. On our initial trip, one of the owners of the hotel, a middle-aged woman, thought I was Turkish and not married to Chieko. She appeared to be very angry with me, but after I figured out why she was upset, I explained that Chieko and I were married, and all was well after that.

We spent a few of our vacations in the historic town of Bursa. The coal-burning city was always smoggy, and in the winter, we saw only the shadows of the men and women who appeared as ghostlike figures making their way along the streets of the city.

Chieko, Daniel, and I stayed in a lovely new hotel that featured modern rooms and a magnificent *haman,* or Turkish bath, where we spent time relaxing in the natural sulfur water. One afternoon, we took a cable car up the snow-covered mountains of Mount Uludag, or as the Greeks called it, Mount Olympus. While riding up the mountain, I thought back to the time when I was at Garfield Elementary School where I imagined what the Greek gods must have seen when they looked down from the mountain to view the mortals, and all that they had created. The scene was just as I had imagined it.

While having a delightful dinner at the hotel, a man from a neighboring table looked over at me and acted like he had just swallowed a cockroach. My guess was he didn't care much for Jews, and I could swear that he was Muammar Gaddafi, but I couldn't be sure. But there was a tasty side to the town, too. Every time we left the city, we would stop at a sweet shop and load up on the candied chestnuts that were produced in Bursa.

During our stay in Bursa, we visited the home of Mustafa Kernal Ataturk (1881-1938), the father of modern Turkey. He wrote that Turkey must look to the West for its future and not the East.

The ancient Blue Mosque was fading into the darkness as dusk enveloped the famous site, and in the city of Istanbul, the calls to prayer were being answered by its male citizens. Chieko and I were walking down a steep cobblestone street when we decided to stop at a very unusual and very unique restaurant for dinner. After we entered the place, we were amazed to find that there weren't any electric lights in the entire restaurant, in its place there were thousands of candles. Once upon a time, it had been a water cistern supplying most of Istanbul with its water supply, but after centuries of lying dormant, the cavernous structure was converted into a lavish restaurant. Constructed of ancient bricks and separated into iron grated booths, the customers dined in the privacy of their private stalls where that ate and drank with a degree of privacy. Both the food and service was nothing short of terrific, the candles were romantic, the classical guitar music soothing, and the wine was both outstanding and inexpensive. Although the place was loaded with hungry patrons, it seemed like we were alone in that fabulous eatery. Our conversation flowed as smooth as a calm sea as we took our time sipping the wine and eating our delicious meal. *En vino veritas!* Yes, we felt very much in love and we were held captive by the romance of the evening. After finishing our dinner, the two of us had another round of wine and some dessert. Chieko and I agreed that it wasn't a place that we would soon forget.

We traveled with another couple, an U.S. Air Force dentist and his wife, Alan and Betsy Hale, to Pamukkale see the famous salt formations and hike around its ancient sites. After roaming around the hills and taking pictures of each other, we went to dinner at the hotel. During the meal, a bus load of Japanese tourists came into the place, and to say the least, they were very subdued. Except for an occasional laugh from one of us, it was so quiet that you could hear a fly scratch himself. That is when I decided to liven things up a bit. When the waiter came over to our table to refresh our drinks, I stretched the truth by about five months and told him it was my birthday. A few minutes later, the waiters brought me a birthday cake complete with candles. When they began singing, it took only a few seconds before the Japanese tourists joined in with the waiters to sing "Happy Birthday." Instantly a party broke out, and for the remainder of the evening, everybody danced and had a great time.

After returning from a shopping trip in Alsancak, the headache inducing stench coming from the Aegean Sea didn't seem all that bad as we approached our apartment building. When we arrived at the front door, just behind us, there were two people speaking Japanese, so we turned around and said *Konnichi Wa* (good afternoon). After chatting for a few minutes, Chieko and I invited them up to our place for some tea and snacks. Comparing the various aspects of Japan and Turkey were among the subjects we talked about. During the course of the conversation, Hiroshi-san told us that he was a movie producer and that he met Yoko-san in London. It must have been love at first sight, because they decided to travel throughout the Middle East together. As the dinner hour approached, we decided to take our new friends to our favorite restaurant in Izmir, so we walked outside onto the First Cordon and hailed a cab to Konak.

While we were enjoying our meal, I noticed that several policemen were milling around in front of the restaurant. I remarked to Chieko, "Maybe there was an automobile accident."

Chieko replied, "Yes, probably. The Turks are terrible drivers."

A few minutes later, four angry and heavily-armed policemen came into the restaurant with guns at the ready. After the men took several steps into the eating establishment, I came to the alarming realization that they were heading straight for our table. The guy with the sergeant's chevrons on his sleeves shouted in a commanding voice, "Who are you? What are you doing here?"

Their tommy guns were pointed right at us, and they were prepared to shoot the damn things if we made any sudden moves. I quickly put my hands up and shouted, "NATO! We are NATO!"

The tough-looking sergeant replied, "Let me see ID." Chieko and I got out our identification cards. "Hmm. What do you do here?"

"I am the president of the American School. And this is my wife," I said.

Then he turned his attention to the Japanese couple.

"Let me see your passports." Without saying a word, they carefully reached into their travel bags and retrieved their travel documents. "Hmm," he mumbled, without giving us a hint of what was happening.

Finally, he ordered his men to lower their weapons while I recovered my wits enough to ask him a question,

"Tell me sergeant. What is the problem?"

The policeman responded, "A couple of Japanese *Sekigun* (Red Army) are in town. And we want to find them."

With that said, he and his men turned around and stormed out of the restaurant.

Following the incident with the police, we said goodbye to the Japanese couple, and they quickly and quietly faded into the Turkish night. "You know," I said, "they told us that they met in London and were now traveling together. Just maybe they were the two Red Army people that the Turkish police were looking for."

The sun settled beyond the horizon, and the Turks were eating and drinking in the numerous restaurants on the First Cordon as Chieko and I, just seven stories above the diners, were in bed reading. Daniel, Michelle, and a friend, were playing with the Ouija board in Daniel's room and all seemed peaceful enough, when suddenly the evening's silence was interrupted by a loud scream. I threw my book down, leaped out of bed, and sprinted to Daniel's room to see what was wrong. At first, I thought someone had broken into the house, but I found out that it was even more ominous. The three of them were playing with the Ouija board when the spirit they had contacted began saying nasty things to Michelle. When she looked down at her thigh to see who was grabbing her, she didn't see anything, but she sure felt it. She screamed and ran out of the room toward the seventh floor balcony. By the time I got to my daughter, Daniel was holding onto her for dear life. Michelle had a look of unmitigated terror in her now pale face, and she was shaking like an old fashioned washing machine. I grabbed her from Daniel and held her in my arms. I felt an evil force between us, but speaking under my breath, I said to whoever or whatever it was, *I am stronger than you. I am stronger than you. So you might as well let go.* Finally, the force let go and Michelle slowly came back to us.

The next day, we went to our Turkish friends and told them about the incident. They told us to place evil eyes in the hallway, rooms, and doorways. After we did this, we no longer had any problems with the bad spirit. A few days later, I gave the Ouija board to one of the teachers, and none of us has ever played with the game again.

While the DoDDS director of personnel was at our school for her annual visit, we went to our favorite Turkish restaurant for lunch. After finishing our meal, we walked down the street discussing a couple of issues pertinent to DoDDS, when Chieko, who was slightly ahead of us at the time, fell victim to a twenty-something year old fellow who had reached down and pinched her on her lovely butt. At first she was so upset that she couldn't speak. Finally, able to talk, she said, "Harvey, did you see that? He pinched me on my rear end!" For some reason, that really bothered me. So without running shoes or a jogging outfit, I chased him down the street. I was uncertain what I would do after I caught him, but I was in excellent running shape, so there was no doubt in my mind that I would soon get my hands on the guy. Two blocks later, I grabbed the poor fellow, and once I had a hold of him, I began pinching his butt and asking him how he liked it? Well, he didn't like it very much, but he did nothing about it during my assault on his pride and his ass.

During our three years in Turkey, Dan graduated high school and spent a year, along with Michelle, going to the University of Maryland in Izmir. After a year, he went back to the United States to enter The Grove Music of School in Los Angeles, but four months later, Daniel dropped out of the music school and enrolled at Sacramento State University. Michelle, who had to be practically dragged out of the house to go to the Izmir Airport, took a plane to Hawaii and found work as a receptionist at the Outrigger Hotel. Later, the beautiful young woman interviewed and was chosen to become a flight attendant for Continental Airlines. As for me, after three years in Turkey, I received a transfer back to Sicily. But this time it was to Comiso.

Italy and Sicily

After boarding a ferry boat from the pier just one block up the street from our former apartment building, we were on our way to Venice. On the main deck of the vessel there was a swimming pool, as well as a scattering of lounge chairs and tables around drinking beer and talking with each other. The ship's passengers looked out at the sea and on the shore at the villagers who politely returned our waves. Along the way to Italy, we hugged the rocky coast of Greece and Yugoslavia as we sailed through the canals and passageways that pressed against the rugged coastline.

Arriving in Venezia, we drove our car off the boat, and after a short stay in Venice, we motored onto the city of Verona. While touring the ancient town, we went to see Romeo and Juliette's famous balcony, and after leaving Verona, we made our way to Aviano Air Force Base for a couple of nights at the on-base lodge. On the following day, we drove forty kilometers to Udine to see our dear friends, Emile and Ellie Mika. After several years at Sigonella, Emile was now the principal of Aviano High School. At his new school, he continued to earn the respect of his teachers and students. While visiting with the Mika's, we met up with our daughter, Michelle, who flew into nearby Trieste to join us on our journey to Sicily.

After my daughter's arrival, and following a final visit with the Emile and Ellie, we began our trek down the peninsula to Sicily.

While shopping for sandwich meat in a small grocery store in Greve, we decided that we liked the town, and that is when we decided to search for a hotel. The first and second hotels were full, but at the third hotel, a customer had just called to cancel his reservations, so we ended up taking his room. The area was known for its production of excellent wines, so that evening, we enjoyed a bottle of the town's famous chianti and consumed a fabulous meal complete with pasta and salad. But before going out to dinner, I went for a run around the outskirts of the town where I sensed many of the same sights and smells as my wine-producing hometown of Napa, California.

The next morning, after having a cappuccino and a *sfogliatellis*, we left Greve and drove to Siena to see the Piazza del Campo, the Duomo and the Palazzo Pubblico. As for the town, it was absolutely stunning. In fact, a few years later, Daniel remained so haunted by the beauty of Siena that he named our lovely granddaughter after the city.

After arriving in Comiso, we stayed at the BOQ for two weeks before being offered on-base housing. In spite of my protests to the Comiso base commander that we wanted to live on the economy, my concerns were ignored. Since there were plenty of new houses that no one had ever lived in, I was given an attractive two-story house at ground zero of the missile site. In case of a nuclear conflict, we would have been vaporized even before I knew there was a war.

Every morning, I would buck the traffic and drive off base for a cappuccino and a sweet roll at my favorite bar in the town of Comiso. After I finished my breakfast, I would drive back on base and go to work. Later in the morning, with my two supply guys, we would sneak off to Vittoria for a late morning coffee.

While principal of Comiso American School, situated on the former German Luftwaffe airfield that had been converted into a missile site, we traveled mostly on the island to the towns of Vittoria, Modica, Catania, and Palermo. On Saturday mornings, we drove into the scenic city of Ragusa, where the ancient houses seemed to be built on top of each other, to stroll around the crowded town and have coffee and lunch. On my bike, nearly everyday after school, I rode through the nearby Sicilian countryside enjoying the view of the many vineyards and orange groves. Occasionally, I'd see a group of Italian bicycle riders and I'd do my best to keep up with them, but they always managed to pull away and leave me in the dust. As for my running, it was mostly confined to jogging around the three mile perimeter of the Italian base.

At the school, we had an American and an Italian supply clerk who were both were amiable and hardworking, but the Italian clerk was young, handsome, and dressed like a prince. As a matter of fact, one of his other jobs was posing for a couple of Italian fashion magazines. The

American was an older fellow and one hell of a nice guy who would do anything for you that wasn't illegal.

One day, while out for a cup of coffee, the Sicilian fellow told Hugh, the American logistics fellow, and I the following story.

A few months ago, I was driving back from visiting my girlfriend in Catania when I became drowsy and veered off the road. As it turned out, I almost hit another car and the near collision knocked me out for a minute or two. The owner of the other car, and his wife, came over to my automobile as angry as a horde of bees. Instead of speaking, I pretended to be unconscious so that I wouldn't have to say anything. The owner was a member of the Mafia, so he pulled out his pistol and he was going to shoot me, but when he pulled back my slumping head, the guy recognized me and decided at the last moment to let me live. Later, I told my father about the incident and he went to the man and his boss to tell them to never touch his son again. The fellow and his capo apologized to my father. But until I married my girlfriend several months later, I took the bus to Catania.

Although the school was only three years old, the powers to be in Washington announced that the American missile site would close in a year. The plan was to have the school end its academic year six weeks earlier than normal, and it was my responsibility to set up a schedule to complete the minimum number of days required to complete the school year. After working with the regional union president, we decided that we would work a certain number of Saturdays. Although the union president endorsed it, the staff didn't like it, but I never got to see it in action because I was on my way a new assignment.

Sardinia

Just off the northeastern coast of Sardinia is the romantic island of La Maddalena. With its beautiful beaches, clear blue water, and the home of Giuseppe Garibaldi, it is well worth the trip. Although a bit complicated to get to, and unless you flew to Olbia about forty minutes away, it took two ferry boats to get the the island. First, there was the overnight ferryboat to the island from Cittavecchia to Sardinia, and then a second boat to La Maddalena.

When we got off the second ferry, only a fifteen-minute ride from the main island, we went to our hotel that was located next to the port. After unpacking, the three of us walked around the picturesque town before going to *La Focacceria*, on *via Garibaldi*, for some oven-baked pizza. La Maddalena was overflowing with tourists from Italy, Sweden, Germany, Denmark, and several other countries, and all of them seemed to be having a great time. Approximately eleven thousand citizens attended its shops, operated a small supermarket, served as baristas at numerous coffee bars, and managed a scattering of restaurants throughout the small tourist town. There was also a market place that sold fresh vegetables, fish, poultry, and meat. Being new to the island, we were impressed by the leisurely pace of the vacationers, as well as the indifference paid to them by the natives. Some of the tourists were barely clothed, but the town's citizens paid little attention to the ubiquitous tourists.

What was left of my summer vacation was spent going to the beach with Daniel where we snuck side glances and took pictures of the topless Scandinavian girls. I managed to get in my daily runs around the island, drink cappuccinos, and read the *Herald Tribune* at the local bars during the leisurely summer break. However, after a few weeks, all the tourists climbed aboard the awaiting ferries, and the island was handed back to the local inhabitants. As for the locals, they were among the stubbornest people on earth, but they were also a very kind and considerate people.

My first thought upon seeing my new school was that it was much smaller than Comiso. That led me to mistaken belief that running the school was going to be a piece of cake. La Maddalena Elementary was a kindergarten through eighth grade school, and when they completed their final year at the school, most of the students transferred to London Central High School.

It was the first day of school, and the kids waited excitedly outside in the entranceway for the doors to open. Finally the bell rang, and like horses at the starting gate, a couple of hundred students ran through the front door knocking down and trampling the little kindergarten and first graders. At first, I could not believe what I was seeing, but after a few seconds, I rushed into the middle of the melee and pulled the little ones out of harms way.

For the next three days, the obstreperous kids waited outside the building until they calmed down enough to go to their classes. This usually took about twenty minutes, but I was going to wait them out no matter how long it took. Ben Franklin wrote: "He that can have patience can have what he wills." Finally, on the fourth day, keeping in mind they were military kids accustomed to quieting down at the movies when the National Anthem was played, I brought out my jam box and played the Star Spangled Banner, then followed it up with the flag salute. Like magic, it worked, and they went to class as quiet as grazing lambs.

From the playground of our school, we could see the nearby island of Corsica, and one of these days, I promised my wife that we were going take a trip over to the French speaking island. A couple of days after Daniel was back on the island for his winter break, we took a boat ride over to the Corsica. It was a pleasant trip as we sailed for one hour on the Mediterranean Sea to the city of Bonifaccio. The walled city protected its residents against its enemies, however, the wall failed them in 1769 when the French conquered the island. Another event that occurred that same year was the birth of Napoleon Bonaparte in the Corsican town of Ajaccio.

We had our outdoor lunch on the French island, and a nice looking girl who was topless underneath her white blouse, took our order. We called her, "Maria," and although she was kept busy with her duties, she had time enough to give an approving glance at Daniel, but the meeting was a fleeting one, and we were soon on our way back to La Maddelena.

A few months later, we returned to Corsica, but this time we took our car with us. Driving through the many villages from Bonifaccio to Ajaccio was both enjoyable and breathtaking. The quaint towns of Porticcio, Tropiano, and Sartene were picturesque, and they possessed a peaceful quality about them. While passing through the various villages, its citizens remained largely indifferent and impervious to changes. As if we were in a cathedral or a museum, we spoke in near whispers.

Ajaccio, with its old concrete buildings, statues, crepe stands, and wide boulevards, was an enchanting and captivating city. Walking around the town of 66,000 people, we toured several places including the Maison Bonaparte where Napoleon Bonaparte was born, and the Cathedrale Ste-Marie.

As a note of interest, the picturesque city was made famous in Guy de Maupassant's, "Vendetta."

A few months later, Chieko and I took the overnight ferryboat to the mainland of Italy to attend the administrator's conference in Livorno. Since we had plenty of leave time, we were going to take a few days to enjoy the country's many pleasures. Leaving La Maddelena four days before the administrators meeting took place, we had three days of pasta, coffee, and wine in sunny Italy. After a good nights sleep, we pulled into Civitavecchia at five o'clock in the morning. Not being a early riser at the time, Chieko was in a foul mood leaving me with that rare opportunity to exercise my marital duties.

"Honey, we can go anywhere you want in Italy. You just name the place, and we are on our way," I said.

She stared at the map and thought about all the places that we could go. Finally, she made up her mind. "Perugia. I want to go to Perugia. I've been hearing about Perugia candy for years," she said.

"Sounds fine to me, my dear. You read the map and I'll drive to Perugia," I said.

Chieko did a superb job reading the map, and four hours later we found ourselves driving into the town of Perugia primed to see the sites and enjoy all that the town had to offer. We parked our car in a parking lot, then we walked through the Rocca Paolina. We had no idea where we going, so we followed everyone to an underground escalator that took us up the inside of a hill and terminated in one of the town's museums. We walked through a roomful of paintings and out onto the street, the Piazza Italia. Overwhelmed by the sweet and unmistakable smell of coffee, we stopped in a bar and had a couple of expressos. After leaving the place, we walked down a cobblestone street where we discovered a small but charming hotel. Most of the time, Chieko preferred larger hotels, so I was surprised when she agreed that the romantic hotel was just right for us. We checked into the small but nicely decorated room, and then we spent the next couple of days enjoying the beautiful sites in and around Perugia.

After two days of celebratory bliss in the capital city of Umbria, we began our drive to Livorno to attend the administrators conference. On the way, we stopped at a restaurant in Castiglione del Lago for lunch. Afterwards, we walked hand-in-hand around its rain soaked streets where I bought a hand-made coffee mug in a ceramic shop.

Leaving Castiglione del Lago, we drove on to Livorno, located on the Ligurian Sea on the western coast of Tuscany. Upon our arrival, we checked into the Hotel Continental, the site of our annual administrators conference. That evening, we had a party at the hotel, and everybody was excited about being back together again. Besides seeing Emile Mika, I was also great being with Gene Merillo, and Andy Branco, who were good friends that shared with me the many joys and hardships of school administration. A fellow runner, Bob Benson, and I did a couple of hard runs together, and I confess to being really challenged by the guy. He sure could run.

Our meetings, for the most part, were fairly boring, but nevertheless, they had their exciting moments. One of them was watching our worldwide director sleep through the sessions. During the sessions, Emile Mika sat next me and wrote funny notes and sketches. One afternoon, I drew a couple of eyes and pasted them over my eyes, then I turned around and made the other sleepy participants roar with laughter.

While having our coffee and eggs at the hotel, we were surprised when the star of over thirty movies, Ben Gazzara, showed up for breakfast. He was staying at our hotel while filming an Italian movie. Speaking in Italian, he would order his very large bodyguard to get another piece of toast, or another cup of coffee. Ben was a friendly guy who seemed pretty much like the rest of us. He made friends with some of principals, and together, they went into Pisa a couple of times.

A few days later, while eating lunch, some of the administrators mentioned that they had gone into Pisa to a place called *Violinos* to listen to a blind fellow play the piano and sing. They said he was terrific and that I should go see him. I didn't bother, but on the last day of the conference, I found out that the guy's name was Andrea Bocelli.

During the third day of the conference, I received a phone call from one of my teachers. It was about a lieutenant commander, and it involved a incident that took place during the first week of school with her son. The clash occurred at the very beginning of the year when a fight broke out between two boys, and in keeping with the school's discipline practice, I suspended both of them. It was during the phone conversation with the teacher that I learned that I had made an enemy out of one of the mothers, the executive officer of the submarine repair base. Without my knowing it, the lieutenant commander had been undermining me with the locally-hired teachers and intimidating the husbands under her command if their wives didn't cooperate. After we left for the administrators' conference, she came to the school and said the navy was taking over the school.

I said to the teacher, "Thank you. I'll take care of it when I get back to La Maddalena."

Upon my return to La Maddalena, I wrote a five-page letter outlining the mutinous action of the officer and addressed it to the commander of the Sixth Fleet. I included a copy of the letter to the base commander, who happened to be a friend of mine. When he received his copy, the captain was very upset with the news that his executive officer had taken such action.

Over the phone, he asked me, "Have you already sent the letter to the Fleet Commander?"

"No," I said. "I thought I would send you a copy first."

"Dr. Getz. This could ruin my career. How about letting me handle it?"

I thought about it for a moment before replying, "All right. I'll take your word as an officer and a gentleman that you will take care of the problem."

The captain canceled the lieutenant commander's transfer to a very plush position, and her career was as good as over. A month later, while on my way to my favorite coffee bar, the lieutenant commander and I saw each other in front of the town market. And if looks could kill, I'd be a dead man!

My days of being an administrator, and all the hassles and joys that came with the position had come to an end. I decided to give up my job as a principal and return to counseling where I could help young people become the best they could be. After letting DoDDS know of my decision to resign, I was offered a position as a guidance counselor at Seoul American High School, but I turned it down and waited for a job on Okinawa. A week later, I received an offer to become a counselor at Kubasaki High School on Okinawa. And with a great of enthusiasm, I accepted the position.

Okinawa

Many years ago, when leaving Okinawa for Germany, my mother-in-law remarked that we would someday return to the island's embrace. As predicated, she was right, and now we were finally back home. We moved into temporary government quarters at the Kue Lodge where we spent much of our time killing cockroaches, visiting friends, and playing my tenor out on the grassy grounds of the lodge, and I continued with my running by jogging up and down the nearby hills. About a month later, after looking at a series of dumps, we finally found a place to live. It was in Hiyagon, and we stayed in the house for seven years. After speaking with several bankers and constantly getting turned down for a home loan, we met a bank official of a local bank at a friend's party. Because of his confidence and friendship, we received a loan and we were able to build a seaside home in the village of Nakadomari.

The transition from administrator to counseling was somewhat uncomfortable at first. I tried to handle a variety of problems that probably should have been resolved by the principal. Things remained that way for about two months until I was finally able to say to a parent, "I think you had better see the principal about it." Shifting the responsibility to someone else felt good, and it became easier each time I did it.

Paul Summers, one of the great jazz and world music players who led several world music groups over the years, and a fellow Altoona High School band member, played a concert in Naha during the fall of 1998. After Paul finished his concert and signed several CD covers, I walked up to greet the brilliant soprano saxophonist. Seeing me on Okinawa was a big surprise, but after he recovered from the shock, he gave me a big hug. While talking to Paul, he said that Jake Dellinger had recently died from a heart attack. The news was a complete shock to me, and to be honest, I figured that someday I would see Jake again and we would laugh together about the old days. But that pleasure was not to be. There are still times, however, when I visualize Jake's smiling face playing his bass fiddle in the Lou Getz And His Melody Men band. Paul Summers and I spent the rest of the evening together at a local jazz club where we talked into the wee hours of the morning about music, and the people from our old home town.

Over the years, we have done a great deal of traveling around different parts of Asia. Shanghai, the largest city in China, is a place that we visited twice over a period of five years. During those trips, we enjoyed seeing places like the Bund, Yu Garden, City God Temple, and Starbucks. The city showed little traces of communism, and it appeared to most outsiders to be somewhat of a capitalist mecca. Through the dense smog, huge skyscrapers rose above the clouds in the crowded city, and they were multiplying like mosquitos in a old tire. German cars, particularly Volkswagens, seemed to be very popular, although bicycles were still the people's choice for transportation. Western fast food places and modern malls with exclusive places like Armani, Hermes, and Cartier's brand shops grew like weeds in a field of bok choy.

While in China, we took a large van to visit several places outside the city of Shanghai. The ancient town of Koshu with its beautiful gardens, and we walked around Mushaku with its lovely but mysterious canals flowing through the heart of the city. Soshu's version of the leaning tower of Pisa was a place where I pissed my way through for a couple of hours. A short time earlier, we had stopped at a teahouse where I unknowingly ordered the kind of tea that caused me to pee every few moments. In Hangzhou, we sailed on a dragon boat around Mao's summer residents, and we walked around Uchin with its row of wooden houses next to the river. There were other places, too, but I don't recall their names.

One evening, we grabbed a cab from our hotel, the Jin Sha, and rode over to the Bun, that was located next to the Huangpu River to spend an evening at the Peace Hotel. Sir Victor Sassoon, a Sephardic Jew, built the hotel in the early part of the twentieth century, and to this day, it remains a very popular place to stay or visit. We were there to have a few beers and listen to a group of musicians who survived the Japanese occupation and the communist revolution. During World War Two, the jazz musicians were not permitted to play their music, so they took their instruments and music to a cave and hid them. The waiting ended in the 1980s when they went to the grotto, broke out their instruments and music and began playing their old fashioned jazz at the Peace Hotel. Chieko and I had a wonderful time drinking and listening to the music being played the old fashioned way by musicians who were historical legends in China.

In 1930, the great playwright, Noel Coward, while ill with influenza, wrote his famous play, "Private Lives," while staying at the Peace Hotel

Thailand was another place that we visited twice over the years. The first time was back in 1970 when I was a guidance counselor at the Singapore American School. I traveled with our superintendent, assistant principal, and the chairperson of the English department, where we attended a five-day conference at the Bangkok American School. We stayed in the luxurious Presidential Suite of the Hilton Hotel, and the four of us enjoyed all the luxuries that came with the suite. Something that bothered me during our stay in Bangkok was that when we went out of the hotel, we were subjected to constant haranguing by taxi drivers to "boom-boom" with the local girls; an industry that made up about fifteen percent of the economy at the time. We refused to engage in those unsavory activities, and while the taxi drivers got a bit annoying we pressed on with the job of keeping our marriages intact. Once the meetings were over for the day, we went out for a few beers and had dinner at the local restaurants. While in Bangkok, I also had the opportunity to see all the food stalls on my boat ride through the Chatucak, the famous outdoor market.

Our last trip was in 2014, when Bangkok was the most visited place in Southeast Asia. We ate some great food at its restaurants and took a bus tour of the outlining area. Following the bus trip, and a tour of the plush gardens at Si Nakhon Kheun Khan Park. We floated back to Bangkok by boat on the Chao Phraya River where we washed down our delicious lunch with a couple of Thai beers. We also visited numerous temples at Ayutthaya, as well as those in Bangkok, including the Wat Arun, Wat Pho, Wat Phra Kaew, and the Jim Thompson House. We also did some window-shopping on the Khao San Road.

As for my musical musical career, it was both an interesting and lucrative experience. I had several jazz groups including the one with clarinetist, Stan Mays, where we played with Jamey Aebersold background tapes. I also had a trio of guitar, bass, and myself on tenor saxophone, as well as a quartet that played in the military clubs. After a while, I grew bored playing in front of mostly disinterested audiences. Now, I play and record in my home studio, and occasionally play a gig.

During my years at Kubasaki, some of my best moments was watching my students march across the stage and become high school graduates. I knew that I had played a role in their graduation from high school, and many of my students were continuing on with their education. Throughout the years, I made many friends at Kubasaki, including David Young, Robert Mastriano, and Ken Gipson, and I worked with some good people over the years. Two guys that standout in my mind were a couple of counselors named Jim Bryan and Howard Strider. Jim was a former Marine officer who once served on Okinawa. He was amazed at how far Okinawa had progressed over the years.

"The girls used to run around in rubber zories, short skirts, and blouses. The boys' noses were always running, and they dressed in hand-me-down clothes," he said.

I recall an incident that Jim told us about when a Marine master sergeant came into his office as mad as hell.

"You said that all my daughter had to do to graduate was take her language arts class," the Master Gunnery Sergeant fumed.

"Yes. I did say that," Jim answered. "However, she had to pass the class first."

"You didn't tell me that part!" The Marine exclaimed.

After retiring, Jim Bryan, an outstanding golfer who won many tournaments on Okinawa, played the courses in Florida for a couple of years before losing his battle with cancer.

Howard Strider was a gentleman who insisted on things going his way. One day when the students had been dismissed, I was walking past his office when I noticed that he was working intently on his computer. I stepped into his office to see what he was doing.

"Dang it! I can't get this darn computer to do what I want it to do," he moaned.

"Let me see if I can get it to work." I said. I fiddled around with the computer for a couple of minutes, then I finally got it to perform the task that Howard was trying to do. "There you go," I said.

"No. That's not HOW I want to do it," he replied. He went back to the computer and continued working well into the evening.

Howard was in the early stages of Alzheimer's' disease. A year later, he retired, and along with his wife, they moved to a condominium in Boston. For a few years, they enjoyed the pleasures of Boston, but after four years, he entered a rest home in the mountains of northern Italy.

Howard Strider sunk deeper into his disease until he passed away after a couple of years at later.

If it is true that we are defined by the choices we make, then I will continue to travel until I am no longer able to do so. Lately, we have been going to mostly places in Japan proper. Tokyo with its Ginza, Sky Tree, Rippongi Hills, Hibiya Park, Tokyo Tower, the Imperial Palace, and scores of other places, are among those locales that I now prefer. Yokohama, Japan's second largest city has its Chinatown, Yamate and Motomachi districts, all interesting and beautiful places to visit. There is Kamakura, with its grand Buddha, and Kumamoto, a very sophisticated city where I wandered around her magnificent castle and downtown areas. Nagasaki, with its famous Peace Park, the old Dutch Trader Colony, Glover Garden, and Mount Inasa, is a quaint city that once hosted traders from the distant Netherlands. Nagasaki, a victim of total devastation by one of the two atom bombs dropped on Japan, has made a complete recovery. The other city that was obliterated, but also made a miraculous rebirth was Hiroshima. Although it was a terrible way to end the war with hundreds of thousands of civilian deaths, they were the last bombs of the Second World War to fall on Japan.

Hakone, Osaka, and Kagoshima are also among the places we visited over the past few years. On our trip to Taiwan, we took a bus tour where we stopped at a hotel with an *Onsen* (bath house), watched an indigenous native dancing exhibition, toured an area where nationalist soldiers dug tunnels into the mountains, and a variety of other places on our four day tour of the island. On our last day, we visited the Chang Kai Chek museum in Taipei.

As for my friends, Erika Geller, the former Landstuhl librarian, married a doctor stationed at the Landstuhl Army Hospital. After he got out of the Army, they moved to Sacramento, California. During her years in California's capital city, we visited with them several times. Erika remained happily married, but eventually an illness took her young life.

My dear friend and former Okinawa roommate, Charlie Higa, had a successful career in the army where he earned a silver star and many other medals as an Army Ranger in Viet Nam. The company commander was considered by his men to be one of the best combat leaders in the war. Higa-san was responsible for many innovations that were integrated into the Rangers, including the berets that his men wore in Viet Nam. Colonel Higa retired several years ago and is living with his wonderful wife, Connie, in South Dakota. He continued to serve his community by volunteering as a football coach and providing chaplain duties at a nearby prison. They have two children, a son and a daughter. Their Korean born daughter, who is married to a Japanese fellow, resides in Tokyo. Their son graduated from West Point and went on to become an airborne officer just like his father.

Susan Francis, the beautiful blond with whom I explored the markets, streets, and alleys of Okinawa with, married a captain in the Special Forces, Tom Bayha. Both continue to be dear friends, and in the summer of 2014, we were fortunate to spend three days visiting with the couple in San Antonio. While there, we hiked along a western trail, purchased a couple of saxophone reeds at a music store, played a few tunes together on a rented tenor saxophone, visited the Alamo, and walked along the city's river front. Tom earned numerous medals for bravery in Viet Nam, including a Bronze Star for Valor, and a Purple Heart. His Special Forces unit had the dubious distinction of having the highest number of casualties in the Viet Nam war. Tom retired as a colonel, then worked for the Sony Corporation in Japan for a few years. Later, he established his own business before retiring in San Antonio. By the way, Tom plays a pretty mean piano.

The destiny of Jean Baumholder led her to a very different and remote place, North Borneo. Jean joined the Peace Corps at the same time that I went overseas to teach on Okinawa. Romance made things easy for the both of us. I met a beautiful and intelligent Japanese girl, and Jean married a fellow she met in the Peace Corps who later went on to become a rocket scientist.

Regarding the guy who tried to throw me into the Shippensburg State College fountain, although I certainly don't regard him as a friend, I ran across him while attending my annual summer National Guard training at Virginia's Camp A.P. Hill. I drove our commanding officer in our unit's jeep to the headquarters building for a meeting, and when I walked into the building, sitting at the front desk was the same guy I had tossed into the water four years earlier. The sergeant recognized me immediately, and if looks could kill, once again, I'd be a dead man.

About a year after leaving Gaeta, I met Rino Agosti in Rome while waiting for yet another airline strike (*sciopero*) to end. For several reasons, including Rino being fired for not keeping logistics records, he absolutely despised the porcine principal who succeeded me. He got another government job at the navy post office, but I believe his hatred for the principal eventually killed him. He was a very proud man who felt humiliated by the principal. A few years ago, I emailed Anna Napolitano, who told me the very sad news that Rino died from cancer about ten years earlier.

Jack Colbert, my old friend from my Altoona days, went on to major in education at Indiana State University of Pennsylvania, and eventually became a principal in Michigan before retiring.

Today, he is a loving grandfather and will always be my pal. Jack lives happily with this wife, and dog, Harry. He still plays his trumpet in community bands in both Michigan and Florida.

Irving "Butch" Kaminski, later in life, lost his sight, but not his vision of ownership and pride. He is now an entrepreneur of a small shop in one of the federal buildings in Washington, DC.

The last time I saw the trombone playing Ronnie O'Brian, was when he was home on leave from the Air Force. The control tower specialist attempted to get to me to enlist in the Air Force after I graduated from college, but I had other plans in mind.

A few months after John Yardley stayed at my place at State College, he moved to Europe where he gained the respect of jazz fans throughout the continent. John recorded several albums with Hog O'Brian, Al Haig, Harold Banter, and several other musicians of note. He performed notably with his old pals, Chet Baker, and Jacques Pelzer, and was a lifetime member of the WDR Big Band in Cologne, Germany. Indeed, it was unfortunate that the jazz fans at Penn State never had the chance to hear him play. John Yardley died in Belgium on April 1, 1991.

Mitchell, and my daughter-in law, Denice, and their three cats, live on Okinawa where they enjoy the many aspects of the Okinawan culture, particularly the East China Sea. Over the years, Mitchell has maintained his sense of humor and, at times, he manages to bring a smile to my aging face. Denice is busy teaching and loving it, while Mitchell keeps himself occupied with his stand up board activities, and teaching elementary school. They live in our apartment complex just a few feet away from our house.

Daniel and Beth are celebrating their lives in Sacramento, California with their children, Siena and Carter. Besides being an excellent student, Siena is a great soccer player, and one of these days, we may see her on the USA Women's soccer team. Carter, with his dry sense of humor, is a interesting fellow who reminds me a bit of myself when I was his age. Daniel, when not playing and singing with his band, or running ten-kilometer races, is selling glass frames and sun glasses to optometrists and stores in Northern California. He also travels yearly to Italy to see his many friends. Beth is an executive with the Marriott Corporation, and is doing very well administrating the comings and goings of the hotel business. And she loves to travel, as well. Beth and Daniel are extremely kind and understanding to their children, and the two of them treat their children with a great deal of love and respect. And that is the ingredient that makes them great parents.

Michelle and Ken have carved out a career in the Navy. As a medical doctor and former submarine officer, he continues to be promoted up through the ranks on a regular basis. In September 2015, he was promoted to the rank of captain, and we are extremely proud of him. They have come a long way together since their first meeting in the Sigonella PX where she worked as a salesgirl, and Ken was on a NROTC cruise in the Mediterranean. Our granddaughters, Hanna and Bella are both very intelligent and beautiful. Hanna looks like her mother, and the unbridled Bella, resembles her father, but is beginning to look a bit like her mother. Both do very well in school where they excel in everything, including music. Hanna plays the piano and sings quite well. Bella loves to dance and make a general nuisance out herself. But I love both of them unconditionally. My daughter, Michelle, continues to be beautiful in every way. I must add that she is an incredible mother, and Ken is a magnificent father.

The sun keeps shining in Honolulu and Yukihiro continues to bring in the coins with his limousine service. Michiko, his lovely wife and a talented artist, recently gave up her bridal preparation business and is now selling her wonderful paintings on the internet. My grandchildren, Sean and Monique are also both doing well. Sean is repairing cars and going to school, while Monique, who is married to Randall Naka, is a computer whiz with the Grumman Corporation in San Diego.

Chieko, Mitchell, Denise, and David Young, held a party for me shortly after I retired from DoDEA at the Renaissance Hotel. The restaurant, along with its excellent food, was full of friends from several schools on Okinawa. I didn't say a whole lot at the time, but I managed to thank them for everything they had done to help make my fifty-two years in education possible.

My Father

Shortly before his death, Dad bemoaned the fact that he never had a childhood. The only break in his work life came when he was when he served as an infantryman in the Army. He underwent the rigors of army training in spite of the fact that most of those fellows he served with were at least ten years younger. He hinted that while he was in the army, he was a victim of anti-Semitism, but he never complained about it. One quiet evening, he was lying in his bunk when he noticed one of the men kept staring at him. A moment later, the soldier jumped from his bed and assaulted my dad. Dad was more than able to take care of himself, and threw the guy onto the floor of the barracks where his buddies subdued the poor fellow. Another time, my dad was an acting sergeant until he asked for a day off to participate in high-holiday services. When he returned from the synagogue, he was no longer an acting sergeant. He was always proud of his service in the Army, and I still remember the time he brought home a couple of soldiers from Texas. Somewhere, there is a picture of the three soldiers at the Fifth Ward bus stop as they waited for it to take them to the railroad station then back to Texas.

Perhaps the most memorable time I had with my dad was when I had missed the band bus to Williamsport. After playing a dance band job the night before the game, I had overslept. When I finally awakened, I realized that I was too late to make the band bus. I was close to panicking when my dad told me to get in my band uniform because he was going to drive me to the game. He cheerfully drove the one hundred miles to the Williamsport stadium, and just as we got there, the band was preparing to march down the field for the opening of the game. Mr. Mariano was very impressed with my dad's gesture, and I will always think of our time together on that wonderful drive to the football game.

My Mother

Perhaps Mother was a bit rambunctious when it came to looking after my well-being, but she always meant well, and that is the difference between being overprotected, and merely guided in a certain direction. But in spite of her intransigent ways, I was as stubborn as she was, so I pretty much did what I wanted anyway. In spite of her tenacious protests, I crossed the clear lines that religions attempted to define and chose girlfriends that she didn't exactly approve of, even the ones she didn't know about. In any case, she loved me, and for that, I am extremely grateful.

A month after our wedding ceremony at the Naha consulate, we made a tape to my parents telling them that we were now married. Not having a tape recorder, my mother went to the downtown Book and Record Shop to listen to the tape. When my Mother got to the part where I told her that I was married, she flipped out in the glass booth and ended up in the hospital for a few days. But after she got to know Chieko, mother came to love her with all of her heart.

Shortly before my mother died, Chieko and I visited with her in a Las Vegas nursing home. As nursing homes go, it was a pretty nice place. When we walked into the house, she was extremely happy and very surprised to see us. Mother was so pleased, that she got up from her chair and danced around it. A couple of days later, when it was time for us to leave, the two of us sat outside on a bench together where she cried in my arms. At that moment, I wanted to take her back to Okinawa, but I knew that it was impossible.

My Brothers and Sister

My brother Lou, bandleader, teacher, motorcycle rider, photographer, bicyclist, and an airplane pilot, and my sister-in-law, Sandy, are gone now. Throughout the years, we got along well, but his behavior towards me was somewhere between the kid that couldn't punch me anymore, and the brother who took charge of my life long enough to get me into college. He was a very bright guy who was able to retire from teaching at a relatively early age and pursue his many interests. Every year, when we returned to the states, I would call him, but he would usually start off our conversation feeling somewhat uncomfortable, but after a minute or two, he would be as friendly as hell. Lou was the leader of Lou Getz and His Melody Men, and he sat near me in the saxophone section of the Altoona High School band. He was a complex man, but I loved my brother.

While we were in Landstuhl, Germany, I received a letter from my brother, Allen, informing me that he was gay. My only choice was to like it or lump it. Since he was my brother and would always be my brother, I decided to like it. After we moved to Napa, Allen and his partner, George, were living in San Francisco, and whenever we went to their house on Steiner Street, I would embrace George then look over at my brother and say, "Oh, how are you, Allen?" This was done in good fun to tease my brother. However, things didn't end well for George, the very gifted and talented young actor, writer, and college professor, later succumbed to AIDS.

Allen is not only my brother, but he is also a fellow who played clarinet in the Altoona High School band, and is also a Penn State graduate. My dear sister, Janet, a woman who has worked hard most of her life, has a belly laugh that I find both amusing and warm. Janet raised two wonderful children, Barbara and Michael, and she is to be highly commended for her efforts. She is now in the real estate business and is doing quite well. Both Allen and Janet are residents of Las Vegas and are enjoying life to its fullest.

San Antonio, Texas

Visiting with Tom and Susan Bayha in San Antonio during the summer of 2014, I surprised the hell out Emile and Ellie Mika. I couldn't get him by e-mail simply because he wasn't checking it. After trying several efforts to contact him, Tom offered to drive me three blocks over to his house to see if he was there. We pulled up in front of his house and while Tom waited in the car, I knocked on the the front door. Emile, who was expecting a book to arrive at any moment, was standing just inside the door waiting for the mail man. When he opened the door, instead of seeing the guy from the post office, he saw me. Emile nearly went into a state of shock, and he was speechless for what seemed like two minutes.

Finally, I broke the silence, "I'm Harvey Getz," I said.

Emile found his voice and said, "I know who the f--k you are!"

We embraced as Ellie peeped around the door to see what the commotion was all about. After finding out who was at their front door, she also gave me a big hug. We talked for a few minutes then Emile invited Tom and I into their house. Both lovely and quite large, their home was tastefully decorated with the finest furnishings. A huge window and glass doors dominated the living room, while a high ceiling, and an incredible staircase leading to the second floor were central to the home. His magnificent paintings decorated the white walls. It was a home worthy of the Mika's. The four of us talked for about twenty-five minutes before promising to return at three o'clock with Chieko.

Later in the day, Chieko and I went to Emile and Ellie's house to enjoy an afternoon of Vino Verde, a slice of delicious strawberry cake, and a great deal of love.

Finally, there is my wife, Chieko, my sweetheart and wonderful companion. She continues to be a beautiful woman in every possible way, and he still manages to turn a head or two when we go out somewhere.

She is kept extremely busy managing her apartments, playing the stock market, and selling health products. Chieko is a member of Soroptimist International, as well as a few other club activities. For several years, she was responsible for the implementation of a charity program that gave millions of dollars to various Okinawan organizations. In spite of her multitude of friends, Chieko-San's biggest job is looking after me. This she does with extraordinary willpower, patience, and unlimited love.

Italy

Although there have been many tales written in this story, you may have forgotten that I promised to reveal the action that kept me from being robbed by the band of gypsies. As you may, or may not recall, Chieko and I were in Firenze (Florence) at the time. We were just about finished taking pictures for the day, when we found ourselves confronted by a band of gypsy girls.

An overly-dressed couple, who were directly behind us, and a poorly clothed group of gypsies walking towards us, decided to make us victims of their slippery fingers. When I saw the dreaded newspaper appear from beneath one of the girl's coats, I knew we were in big trouble. As they approached, I had a surprise for them. Borrowing my moves, with apologies to Bruce Lee, I began kicking and howling at the gypsies. The girls were so surprised by my actions that they backed off from their attack. The would-be thieves were definitely befuddled, and that is when they made eye contact with the well-dressed couple standing behind us. The fellow gave the sign for them to disappear because I was either crazy, or I knew karate and was prepared to use it. Now, my new video camera and our money were safe. Meanwhile, the young man and woman crossed the street and quickly disappeared into the crowd of tourists. With the marauding band of thieves now gone, we breathed a sigh of relief, then Chieko and I headed back to the train for Livorno.

Epilogue

The dilapidated market reminded me of those not so long ago times when it was common for every town and village in Okinawa to have such places. Resting on the warped wooden shelves were cans of Spam, soap, aftershave lotion, eggs, white radishes, sweet potatoes, carrots, and a couple of other items. Doing their best to brighten the darkness of the market was a display of flowery cotton dresses that must have been there since the village of Ishikawa was a war refugee camp.

Looking at the small restaurant with an exterior whose best days were many moons ago, I said to Chieko, "I bet the *soki soba* is really good in this place."

"Why would you want to eat in an old place like this?" Said my wife who fancied places like the Renaissance Hotel where we ate surrounded by elegance and great food.

"Because I think it would be fun," I replied.

Looking through the slightly dirty window, we could see the wall menu. "Look," I remarked, "Everything is at least a hundred yen cheaper than what we normally pay. Besides, I wouldn't be surprised if it's really good."

"Well, we can try it." My wife reluctantly relented.

"Half the tables are occupied, so it must be pretty good," I assured her.

"Yes, that is true. But there are only two tables," she casually observed.

Squeezing our way past the large aluminum *Oden* cooker, we made our way to the other table. Like a kid on a sliding board, I almost skidded off the slanted folding chair as we sat down to be served. Both of us laughed as we'd braced our legs firmly onto the concrete floor to prevent our backsides from sliding off the chairs.

The rotund woman wiggled between the labyrinth of clutter to get to our small table to serve us green tea and take our order. Chieko chose *soki soba* and I ordered fried noodles. A few minutes later, she returned with our order. After tasting the soup, Chieko remarked, "Your noodle soup is very good. It certainly has the taste of *Ishikawa soba.*

"*Domo arigato,*" replied the elderly woman.

At the other table were two middle-aged men, and on their uniforms they had the name of the vending machine company where they worked. "*Konnicha wa,*" they smiled. They were Okinawan smiles.

We returned their greeting with a "good afternoon" of our own. Many Okinawans believe that once people have greeted each other, they become brothers and sisters. It is called *Icariba chode,*

The two fellows, who initially believed that Chieko was from Tokyo, and not Okinawa, switched from the Japanese language to *Hogen* after my wife convinced them that she born in nearby Nakadomari. Hadn't my wife interpreted the older of the two men's tale of his youthful encounter with the American soldiers, I wouldn't have understood a word they said. Anyway, the story was in interesting one, and he held our interest throughout the tale.

When the Americans practiced their war training in the fields surrounding our small farm, I found it enjoyable. Almost like a war movie or something. They would crawl over the sweet potatoes, and splash through the rice paddies pretending to shoot each other. When it got too hot or rainy, they'd stop their games and join their "enemies" for lunch and hot coffee. My big brother and I would stand by and watch them until they finally offered us some of their food. I really liked the Spam, but the hot dogs and beans were my favorite.

The best part of watching them play war was when the GI's jumped out their airplanes and parachuted down onto the field. If we were quick about it, we could get a few things that had been dropped from the airplane. One day, we rushed onto the landing zone to grab one of the boxes, as well as the parachute. Mother used the beautiful silk material to make dresses for our little sisters. Although a couple of soldiers, who were still floating down to earth, saw us, they didn't shoot or yell at us. My guess was that they really didn't care. But we had to be careful because the biggest danger was if one of those boxes hit you on the head, you would be dead for sure. The box and parachute we appropriated were small, but a little heavy. Together, my brother and I managed to get back to our house with our contraband before the soldiers could stop us. Our dear mother became very excited when she saw what we had brought from the field.

After carefully folding the parachute and hiding it in the closet, she tore open the box.

After mother finished opening the box, we immediately saw a couple of dozen light brown rectangular bars.

"*That is soap. It is what they call Castile soap. My sons, this is a very expensive black market item. Your father will be very pleased to see how well you boys have done today!*

I felt a real sense of pride as I peeked into the box at the soap. No doubt about it, father will be very happy.

"*Tonight, after his bath, your father will be as clean as a shaved white radish!*" *Mother exclaimed.*

That night, the whole family watched as father scrubbed himself between his fingers and toes, his back, face, and his short but muscular legs. He also washed his hair with the soap, but to our disappointment, there wasn't a bubble anywhere.

"*Perhaps there is something wrong with the washcloth. Tomorrow night, I'll use your mother's soft cloth,*" *he said.*

It was the following day that my uncle stopped by the house for a visit. While there, my father told him about the soap that wouldn't bubble.

"*Well, let me see the soap,*" *my uncle requested.*

Father opened the box and showed the soap to his brother. My uncle's eyes grew as large as apples when he saw what was in the carton. After staring at the bars for what seemed like an eternity, he roared with laughter. Surprised by whatever my uncle thought was funny, my father said, "Brother, what's wrong with you? Have you gone mad?"

Gathering himself back together, my uncle took a bar of soap from the box and took a whiff of the brown bar.

"*What are you doing?*" *Mother asked.*

"*Just making sure,*" *my uncle replied.*

"*Sure of what?*" *My father inquired.*

"*Dear brother. I know why you can't get any suds when you wash with this soap.*"

"*And why not?*" *Father asked.*

Uncle Tatsuo pressed his hands together and stopped laughing long enough to tell us about the brown bars. "Those rectangular bars that you thought were for cleaning yourself are blocks of American cheddar cheese!"

"Wow!" I said. "That was a really good story. I guess if you had never seen cheddar cheese before, a guy might think it was soap," I laughed.

The two gentlemen from the vending machine company were now finished with the story and their noodle soup. They said a warm *sayonara,* then departed from the old restaurant.

"You know, Chieko. I really love this place.

My wife looked over at the stack of empty boxes and the ancient oven that was stored in the corner. "Do you mean this old restaurant?"

"No. I mean Okinawa. I love this place.

A Few Words To The Readers

I hope that you enjoyed the many stories about the kid who walked down Altoona's Eighteen Street with his mother in search of a couple pairs of rationed nylon stockings. By the way, if you visit Italy, and I hope you do, be on the lookout for those thieving newspaper-carrying gypsies.

Dedication

This book is dedicated to my wife and children who endured, with relative pleasure, the challenges of traveling and living abroad. They did it without complaint, and were as thrilled as I was whenever we received transfers to new and interesting places. Now with kids of their own, they travel the world seeking out the exciting countries that occupy our shrinking planet.

Harvey P. Getz
Okinawa, Japan
July 2016

Printed in the United States
By Bookmasters